Spooky LIVERPOOL

"Spooky Liverpool" is published by:

Trinity Mirror NW²

Trinity Mirror North West & North Wales
PO Box 48
Old Hall Street,
Liverpool L69 3EB

Trinity Mirror Sport Media Executive Editor:
Ken Rogers

Design / production:
Daisy Dutton, Jonathan Low, Emma Smart

ISBN 978 1 905266 42 5

CONTENTS

FOREWORD

I first encountered Billy Roberts via a Jiffy bag. You know, one of those padded envelopes that always brings a surprise.

I didn't realise, fifteen years ago in 1992, that the biography that tumbled out of the package would start a strong friendship.

I first phoned the smiling author at his home and introduced myself with the same gag I have been using ever since: "Hello, Billy, it's the ECHO. I guess you knew we'd be calling." He laughed with an infectious chuckle. And he still laughs when such a remark is made, even though he has heard it all before.

Billy has lived and worked with the other side (and I don't mean Birkenhead) all his life. In our first interview he talked about his Indian spirit guide and his time spent as a rock musician when he went on the road in the 60s. He told me of childhood experiences, dealings with poltergeists and other ghostly goings on.

As a sceptical journalist, I was fascinated when Billy told me things about myself that only I knew – even though I had never met the man. When the article was finished I recall sending it to Billy with a note attached. A while later he sent me a thank you letter with a character analysis of ME which was, as we Liverpudlians say, uncannily 'spot on' – he had put together the profile from my own fair handwriting.

I have seen Billy perform in front of thousands and been amazed that he was so alone up there on stage with just a table and jug of water, only the spirits there to help him. And they never seemed to fail him.

Billy's reputation in the UK and abroad is strong and he is much-in-demand for TV and radio. He has an acute ability to make people feel at ease and his cheery nature and philosophy make you want to meet him time and again.

He is also a prolific writer, too, having penned technical books about his craft but this book is different... cue music from the Twilight Zone.

Here Billy tells tales of Spooky Liverpool – and if anyone knows about the capital of haunting, then it is this ghost hunter.

I once spent a night in a jail cell at St George's Hall for charity and Billy was the ghostbuster guest of honour. He revealed many facts about the famous building that he couldn't possibly have known. He also said a young urchin was sitting by my side, which was news to me, as I couldn't see anyone.

I remember making my excuses and leaving.

Everyone likes a good ghost story and there are plenty of spine-chilling tales here to dip into, including the Vanishing Couple, The Lady of Light and Billy's sojourns into Liverpool's haunted theatres.

Billy, I now await the arrival of my own signed copy, tumbling out of a Jiffy bag... just like that first magical encounter all those years ago. Then again you probably already know that.

PETER GRANT
LIVERPOOL ECHO
MAY 2007

INTRODUCTION

Today the paranormal is attracting a great deal of interest from people from all walks of life. Some universities are even including it in their educational curriculum, giving the whole subject more credibility.

In the past though, anything to do with the paranormal was viewed with disdain and cynicism and, more often than not, associated with 'certain kinds of people'. Today, however, views have changed, and many people are often curious enough to buy at least one book on the subject. In fact, when put on the spot, even the most sceptical person will admit to having had a paranormal experience at some time in his or her life. "I don't believe in anything like that!" the sceptic will affirm. "But there was one occasion…"

As a professional medium and paranormal investigator I have to explore all sorts of paranormal phenomena and frequently find myself in some very frightening situations. Dealing with people who are possessed is one thing, but having to face an extremely aggressive poltergeist is another.

At least with people you can see what they are doing and where they are coming from. Poltergeists are very often an unknown quantity, and by their very nature are always unpredictable.

I am not one of those mediums who attributes every commonplace phenomenon to the intervention of discarnate spirits. Over the years I have become extremely sceptical and have evolved a very cynical attitude towards the paranormal. As far as I am concerned, 'seeing is most certainly believing'. To actually be in a room where furniture is being thrown around violently by invisible hands, and where the moans and groans of disembodied voices resound from wall to wall, is believe me quite frightening, regardless of whether or not one is mediumistically inclined.

It would be silly to say I am not afraid, because I am and always have been. As a child I was so afraid of the dark I could not sleep without the dull glow of a nightlight in the bedroom. Even then the flickering light would create its own demons, which always lurked in the shadowy corners of the room.

Life as a child was quite miserable for me, particularly at night when I had to go to bed. Even pulling the covers over my head did not shut out the shadowy forms that danced teasingly around the dully lit bedroom. I can't say that sleep brought me solace – I was always pleased to see the first signs of sunlight slowly filter through the window come the morning. Little wonder I was always falling asleep at my desk in school. By home time I was so exhausted I was always ready for bed.

Ever since I was a child I have had ghostly encounters of one kind or another. Right up until the age of ten I thought that everyone was the same as me. Seeing so-called 'dead' people was commonplace to me and, as a consequence, I am now certain I sustained a great deal of emotional and psychological damage.

Sometime around the age of nine I was referred to a child psychologist for assessment. The kind and understanding lady doctor was correct with her psychological diagnosis – I was sensitive, insecure and extremely creative with a very vivid imagination. But her prognosis was completely incorrect: she said I would grow out of it in time. She was wrong!

Today I accept that there is an incredible fascination with the paranormal and also appreciate that what is part of everyday life for me may be of great interest to my readers.

For this very reason I have taken great pains to bring together the most interesting and spine-chilling stories that I think culminate into a gripping read.

I have been personally involved in many of the listed cases and have meticulously researched most of them. Some may be a little hard for you to believe, but I do hope you will enjoy reading this book as much as I enjoyed writing for you.

1

THE GHOSTS OF BINNS ROAD

As I turned off Edge Lane into Binns Road, although now quite desolate, the ghosts of years gone by still sent a shiver of excitement down my spine.

This was the actual place where my vast collection of Dinky cars as a child was made, I quietly reminded myself, as each model passed nostalgically through my mind. Although the Meccano factory has long since gone, its memory still casts an immense shadow the full length of Binns Road, but is perhaps only apparent to all those to whom the Dinky toy still brings that familiar rush of excitement. However, as well as the ghosts of enjoyment and the clouds of excitement that hover over the whole area of Binns Road, there is also the deep resonating throb of terror that echoes across the desolate stretch of waste land opposite Crawford's old biscuit factory.

It was there, in a terraced cottage, that a devoted father, traumatised by depression, murdered his two young children in a frenzied attack. He took them upstairs and after slitting their throats, patiently awaited his wife's return with their youngest child. It was his intention to include them also in the macabre scenario, which he would then conclude by taking his own life.

However, his plan was thwarted when his wife returned home with a friend whom she had invited for a cup of tea. Determined to complete the dastardly act, he waited quietly in the bedroom for his wife's friend to leave.

The two women sat gossiping, completely unaware of the fact that the two young children were lying dead upstairs.

In the meantime, whilst the neighbour sipped her tea, blood had seeped through the ceiling and began dripping onto the woman's face and into her cup. The two women immediately ran hysterically with the young child from the house and within twenty minutes the police had arrived. By that time though the husband had committed suicide by slitting his own throat. The upstairs room was a veritable bloodbath – a macabre sight that reduced one of the policemen at the scene to tears.

The house lay empty for some time before finally being let to a young couple. Although the blood stains on the ceiling had been neatly concealed, there were still some brown marks visible. The young couple were completely unaware of the brutal killings, and so immediately set about decorating the house. However, no matter how many times they painted the ceiling, the red stains showed, each time becoming more vivid and clearly defined. They tried papering the ceiling, but still the stains were visible.

One morning the woman got up early to make a cup of tea for her husband and was horrified to see blood dripping from the ceiling. No matter how many times they covered the ceiling the blood still came through the paper and dripped onto the floor. This phenomenon was accompanied by the muffled sounds of children's voices echoing through the house in the middle of the night. As soon as the young couple discovered exactly what had taken place in the house, they immediately moved out. Everyone who lived in the house experienced the same phenomena, right up until the day it was demolished some time in the seventies.

Billy says: Demolishing the bricks and mortar does not in any way eradicate the paranormal activity.
The anguish and emotional trauma is impregnated into the psychic atmosphere, and so anything built upon that particular ground would also experience the same paranormal disturbance.

2

THE MAN WHO WENT TO HIS OWN FUNERAL

Joe Francis's death did not surprise anyone who had known him. He smoked eighty cigarettes a day and the amount of alcohol he consumed in a week had greatly increased over the past twelve months. "It's me only enjoyment!" he had always said. "Besides, you've got to die of something, haven't ya?"

Although Joe had a family, he was a loner and never bothered with anyone. He lived in a one-bedroomed flat in Sandown Lane and he drank in the Bellevue in Picton Road. Alf Swain, Joe's oldest friend, had always joked that it was the pub that kept Joe alive.

One fateful day, Joe was found dead in his flat of a massive heart attack, they said. Apart from Alf Swain and his wife and Joe's three daughters and their husbands, no one else came to the funeral.

Alf had grown up with Joe in Wavertree and had gone to the same school, Sefton Park. They had both joined the army together and fought in France in the war. Although Alf knew that Joe was better off now, he also knew that he would miss him – his old drinking mate. He felt so sad, but more for himself than for Joe.

It was a cold blustery day and Alf and his wife Peggy sat at the back of the chapel watching as Joe's coffin was carried in. Alf leaned over to whisper something to his wife, when he realised that someone had sat down in front of them. Alf raised his brows and gave his wife a curious glance.

They had both thought it very strange that the man had sat so close to them when the chapel was nearly empty. Alf knew all of Joe's drinking cronies, he wondered who the man was. He looked in his mid thirties and was smartly dressed, but both Alf and Peggy thought it very strange that he never moved at all during the service but just sat staring blankly towards the front of the chapel. He didn't even bother to stand when requested to do so by the minister. In fact, he hardly moved at all during the ceremony.

It wasn't until the service was over and everyone had got up to leave that the stranger turned to face Alf and Peggy. He was smiling knowingly at them and then said in a low voice: "See ya' Alf lad!" Then he left the church without saying another word. Peggy could see that Alf's face was pale and for a few moments he was unable to speak.

"Are you alright love?" she asked, placing a concerned hand on his arm. "Sit down for a moment."

"No, I'm alright," he said. The colour suddenly returning to his cheeks and he smiled. "You'll never guess who that was? I've just realised."

"Who?" she answered quizzically. "He must be one of Joe's family. He had that look about him."

"That was Joe!" he grinned. "That was Joe when he was younger."

"Don't be stupid!" she said, thinking that her husband was suffering from delayed shock. "Joe's dead! Don't you remember, that's why we're here? Let's get you home."

"It was him I'm telling you," he insisted, as Peggy gently hurried him from the chapel. She suddenly stopped to retrieve something from where the stranger had been sitting.

"What's this?" she muttered, holding it to her face for closer inspection. It was an old photograph of two young soldiers sitting outside a French cafe drinking beer. Peggy's mouth suddenly fell open when she realised who the soldiers actually were. "This is you!" she declared. "You and..." she stopped.

"Me and Joe," Alf grinned. "This is me and my mate Joe. He must've come to say goodbye."

Billy says: This phenomenon is more common than we might imagine. In fact, similar stories have been related to me by people from all over the country. They had seen the person whose funeral they were attending, standing with other ghostly figures as the coffin disappeared behind the curtains in the crematorium.

3

THE GHOST OF 32 HIGH STREET

The Marland family moved in to 32 High Street, Wavertree, just in time for Christmas. Lilly and Leo always liked to have their family and friends around at least once over the festive period for the proverbial 'do', as the get-together was called.

Number 32 is one of a row of listed terraced houses, probably built around the 18th century. Although it does not look any different from the other houses on that block, I have been assured that at some point within the past 150 years it was most definitely a place of worship, even though the façade of the house does not bear witness to this fact.

It was Christmas in the mid sixties and, as was usual every Boxing Night, friends had been invited back to number 32 for the obligatory drink and to continue with the festivities. Whilst everyone was downstairs drinking and making merry, John Miller, one of the partygoers, made his way up to the bathroom.

On his way back downstairs he passed a little old lady making her way along the landing. She seemed to be attired in old-fashioned clothes and smiled at him as she walked by. "Alright, ma," he said as she passed him. "Are you not joining us downstairs?" The old lady grinned and placed a friendly hand upon his shoulder and shook her head as she continued to make her way down the narrow landing. Before he made his way back to the party he glanced back but the old woman had gone, disappeared into a room, he decided.

Thinking no more about it he went back into the living room. By now everyone was singing and having a good time. "I thought you'd got lost," said Lilly. "Help yourself to a drink."

"I've just been speaking to your mother upstairs," he went on. "She wouldn't come down for a drink."

Lilly looked at him quizzically. "What do you mean? My mother's dead! And there's no one upstairs." She suddenly stopped to brush something from his shoulder. "What's that?" she said curiously. On closer inspection Lilly could see that there was a white handprint on his shoulder. She couldn't remove it no matter how hard she tried.

"The lady touched me," said John.

They both went upstairs to investigate but as Lilly had suspected there was no one there.

"She walked along there," he explained, indicating with his hand. "Towards that room."

"There's no room there," retorted Lilly, "just a blank wall. You've seen a ghost!"

It wasn't until a few days later that Lilly's husband Leo took a look at the wall and discovered that there had in fact once been a door there. After making further enquires he found out that there had been another room there but this had long since gone.

The Marland family saw the old lady many times after that, and also discovered that she had lived in the house over a hundred years ago. The house is still there, and so too is the old woman.

Billy says: The fact that the old lady had walked through the wall where a door had been is evidence that she was seeing the house as it had been when she lived there. It is possible to change the structure of the house, but the subtle nature cannot be altered and will always remain the same to its spirit inhabitants. Spirit people often remain in the same house that they lived in when they were physically alive, but still see it as it was in their own time, regardless of what structural changes have been made.

4

MY GHOSTLY EXPERIENCES

In the early years of my work as a medium, I travelled the country demonstrating my mediumistic abilities in Spiritualist churches.

I must have visited every Spiritualist church in every town and city and, like most mediums, travelled in hail, rain or snow. One of my favourite spiritual centres was in Old Orchard Street, Bath. This was an old Georgian house in a narrow cobbled street. Visiting mediums were allowed to stay in the apartment above the church. This meant that the stay was more comfortable and there was no travelling involved to get to the centre each day.

There was an extremely spacious lounge in the apartment, with two large Georgian windows overlooking a communal square.

I was sitting one autumnal Sunday afternoon tinkling on the piano, somewhat mesmerised by the sunlight flooding the room, encouraging my thoughts to drift. Although I was in the apartment alone I suddenly became aware of someone standing behind me. I knew that the entrance to the apartment was over to my left, and as I had a clear view of the door I knew no one had come into the room. I felt my skin tingle and the hairs on the back of my neck stand up.

I swung round to catch a glimpse of two ladies in long dresses walking across the room. I rose quickly from the chair, and almost simultaneously the apparitions disintegrated into nothingness.

Thinking no more about the experiences I got myself ready for the evening's service in the sanctuary below. Once the service had finished and all the pleasantries were out of the way, I made my way upstairs to the flat. By now I was extremely exhausted and just wanted to go to bed.

No sooner had my head touched the pillow than I fell into a deep sleep. It must have been around three in the morning when something woke me up. The room was in darkness and I could hear voices coming from the adjacent lounge. As I knew that I was the only one in the building I began to feel a little anxious. I reluctantly climbed from my bed and moved slowly to the door. Opening it quietly I peeped into the lounge. Although it was the dead of night, the room appeared to be flooded with light.

I couldn't believe my eyes. There were people attired in 18th century clothes sitting around the room drinking and laughing. Their merriment echoed loudly throughout the whole building and I was certain that the inhabitants of the adjacent houses would soon complain. Suddenly the uninvited guests disappeared without warning and I watched with amazement as the room fell once again into darkness.

Although I do not scare easily I found it very difficult to sleep after that experience. The following day I couldn't wait to tell the president of the sanctuary all about the ghostly experience. However, to my amazement she was not at all surprised.

"Men and woman in 18th century clothes?" she smiled. "This place used to be a brothel," she continued. "It used to be called The Pineapple Inn. Well-to-do businessmen and even politicians used to journey from London to visit the ladies here. You see, nobody would recognise them so far from the hustle and bustle of their own city. The Pineapple Inn was well known to the gentry of the 18th century."

She went on to tell me that many people had seen the ghostly visitors. Needless to say I never slept with the light off after that.

QUEENIE NIXON AND THE FACES OF THE DEAD

During the early years of my work as a medium I used to visit as many veteran mediums as I could, primarily for the experience. I had heard so much about world-renowned transfiguration and trance medium, Queenie Nixon, and was fortunate to have a private consultation with her on one of the rare occasions she visited Liverpool.

Her private consultations were conducted whilst she was in deep trance, and so this made the experience even more exciting.

When I entered the room where the consultation was to take place I was rather surprised to see this middle aged lady sitting bolt upright in the chair. I had been told that Queenie Nixon was quite elderly, and so I had expected the woman who greeted me to be much older than she appeared.

I sat in awe of this well-spoken lady as she told me that my father, Albert Roberts was with me. "He used to work with steam wagons!" she said. This was correct. One time my father owned a steam wagon haulage business. In fact, he was quite enthusiastic about steam wagons.

"He's concerned about your mother's back and legs," she went on. "He says that your mother's suffering with sciatica." That was also correct. I was totally amazed. And when she told me that I was named after my uncle Billy who was killed in Burma in the Second World War, I just couldn't believe it. I was speechless. She was silent for a few moments, and sat there very still. I gazed at Queenie Nixon nervously, not knowing what exactly to expect. As I looked at the lady's face it metamorphosed into my father's face. I couldn't believe what I was seeing as he smiled. He only transfigured on the medium's face for a brief moment, and then he was gone! She continued to sit quietly, not moving a single muscle or nerve, and then it happened again. I saw the strong, heavy features of a lady transfigure over the medium's face. Although I did not realise it at that moment, it was my grandmother who had died six months before I was born. I was speechless and could feel the temperature in the room drop considerably. Then, just like before, the face disappeared, leaving the medium sitting quietly once again.

A few moments elapsed, before I realised that my consultation had come to an end.

The medium concluded the reading by saying: "I would like you to stay whilst I bring my lady back." Although I agreed, I had no idea what to expect. My eyes moved nervously about the room, half expecting someone to walk through the wall. I was still spellbound and didn't know what to think about it all. However, suddenly there was a loud swishing sound behind me. It reached a piercing crescendo as it passed me, then suddenly resounded all over the room as it disappeared somewhere inside the medium. As the sound faded into nothingness the medium suddenly looked much older. Her face now appeared very wrinkled and she looked, to all intents and purposes, like a completely different woman sitting in front of me. Her eyes were now closed as though she was in a deep sleep. I felt a shiver down my spine and my heart missed several beats. The woman's eyes suddenly opened and she spoke to me in a broad Derbyshire accent. "Thank you for waiting," she said in a quiet, polite voice. "Was it good?"

"Yes!" I stuttered nervously, with a feeling as though I was speaking to another person and not the medium who had given me the half-hour consultation. "It was very good." I didn't know what else to say.

"Good!" she said. "Now I'm dying for a cup of tea."

She rose from the chair and made her way gingerly towards the door. She was small and not at all straight like the person in whose company I had just spent the last half an hour.

I watched Queenie Nixon as she slowly descended the stairs towards the kitchen below. I was spellbound and amazed by all the things she had told me. As she reached the foot of the stairs she turned to face me. "I have just been told to tell you Pepe will soon be going to join his dad." Then she turned and disappeared through the door.

Pepe was my mother's elderly poodle. He in fact died some weeks later of kidney failure.

IVOR JAMES AND THE PSYCHIC DRAWING

Although frequently ridiculed by sceptics, the subject of spirit guides has always been an integral part of my work as a medium, and whether you chose to call them spirit guides or guardian angels, I have never doubted their existence for one single moment.

Contrary to popular belief, spirit guides are not just ghostly North American Indians who appear with arms folded to spiritualist mediums in the séance room, they are spirit manifestations who help and guide us through the more turbulent parts of our lives.

In fact, since I was three years old I have been acquainted with a spirit guide I called Tall Pine, a Native American who frequently visited me when I was alone. Tall Pine was an extremely tall and effeminate plainsman who watched over me and kept me entertained.

He was not the archetypal Indian of Hollywood westerns, and never appeared to me with a feathered head dress or attired in traditional Indian clothes. On the contrary TP, as he was affectionately known, was simply clad in a grey blanket and woven cloth trousers with moccasins. His hair was long and fell in two plaits, one on either shoulder. I was the only one who could see Tall Pine, and I knew everything about him.

Just before I began working as a medium, I had a consultation with an international Scottish medium by the name of Mary Duffy, (now deceased) who confirmed, in detail, exactly what Tall Pine looked like.

I needed more confirmation to prove to myself that I was being guided and that Tall Pine was not something I had created in my own imagination as a child. "If you get the chance to see a renowned psychic artist," Mary Duffy began, "Tall Pine will make sure you have a drawing of him. Then you will know he is really there."

A psychic artist is a medium who has the ability to sketch what other mediums can see. This was exactly what I needed.

Ivor James (now deceased) was one of the world's greatest psychic artists and also an expert in the field of the paranormal. I was lucky to be given an appointment with Ivor when he visited Liverpool. At this point all my faith and belief in my work as a medium was dependent upon the sketch that Ivor James produced or did not produce for me.

When I entered the little room where Ivor James was working, I was extremely nervous and my heart was pounding. I was surprised to see Ivor already sketching away as I walked into the room. He was looking down as he was sketching, and I could hear the sound of his pencil scratching the surface of the paper as he produced the image. I just prayed that it was going to be a sketch of Tall Pine and not the face of someone I had never known.

"You know who I am drawing?" He mumbled, raising his eyes over his bi-focals to look at me.

"I hope so," I stuttered nervously and, before I could say another word, Ivor James had signed his finished work and was holding it in front of me. I gasped a sigh of complete relief as Tall Pine's gaunt features looked out from the paper.

"That's Tall Pine!" I murmured excitedly, as I looked at the finely detailed sketch. "Tall Pine."

Ivor James just smiled knowingly at me, a look of sheer pleasure dawning across his face. I left the room without another word being spoken. I was so happy to have the sketch I was holding in my hands. Tall Pine's framed sketch today hangs in a place of pride in my study at home. He still helps me with my work. The sad thing is, I am getting older and Tall Pine is not!

THE GHOSTLY STABLE

Sometime in the mid-sixties I found myself hitching with two friends through Wales where I had been playing with my band. We found ourselves stranded late at night in Prestatyn with nowhere to sleep for the night.

I asked a guy on his way home from a night out at the pub if he knew of any hotels or boarding houses in the area and as it was so late he suggested that we spend the night with him. The only thing was he lived in a disused stable on the farm where he worked. We had no choice, so we graciously accepted.

Although very sparse with only a blanket or two to sleep on, it was a fairly warm and dry place to rest our heads until morning, and for this my friends and I were grateful.

Our host also apologised for the mess, and said that there had been a fire there some weeks before and this was the reason why everything was in such disarray.

He then went on to explain that the stable was haunted and that in the early hours of the morning the sound of a chain could be heard beating against an extremely distressed horse. Our host was quite nonchalant about the whole ghostly tale, and then settled himself down to sleep.

Sure enough as he had said, we woke up around 3am to the ghostly sounds of a distressed horse, rearing on its hind legs and neighing, as the clanking of a chain echoed eerily between the empty stable walls.

The room we had been sleeping in was divided from the main part of the stable by a crudely constructed wooden partition. The three of us quickly went to investigate the ghostly sounds, only to witness old newspapers, straw and soil being thrown all over the place. Even though the cacophony of chilling disembodied sounds continued, the stable itself was absolutely empty. Although we hadn't noticed it then, our host had gone.

We looked everywhere to thank him for his hospitality, but he was nowhere to be found. Needless to say we didn't hang around very long and vacated the stable as quickly as we could.

Some weeks later I returned to Prestatyn with some friends, hoping to show them exactly where we encountered the ghostly commotion of the horse being beaten to death.

To my great surprise the stable had disappeared completely. I made a few enquiries in the village to be told that there hadn't been a stable there for a long time – it had been destroyed in a fire forty years before.

My Schoolfriend Came To Say Goodbye

Being a medium I suppose one would expect me to have had more than my fair share of extraordinary experiences but for some reason they appeared far more meaningful when I was a child than they do today.

Aged nine, I was a pupil at Underlea school in Aigburth when I befriended a boy called Terrence Davies, who was always getting into trouble. Although he bullied and terrorised the other kids, Terry was extremely protective towards me.

He looked fairly healthy in comparison to other children at the school but I always had a strong feeling that he was in fact quite poorly.

We'd just started school after the Christmas holidays and I was looking forward to seeing Terry again. He wasn't there and the teacher told me that my friend wasn't too well and that he would probably be off school for at least a week.

In fact, he was off school for three weeks, and when he came back on the Monday morning I made a dash to greet him, but something stopped me in my tracks.

Terry was surrounded by a very dark, grey cloud. He was ashen faced and seemed distant, just like a stranger. He never came near me all that day and the following morning at assembly the headmaster announced that Terrence Davies had passed away on the Sunday night, the night before I had seen him at school.

It never occurred to me that nobody else had mentioned seeing him on the Monday at school. What I couldn't understand was why he seemed distant like a stranger – not like my friend at all.

My friend did not look happy but I am quite sure now that he only returned to school on that Monday morning to say goodbye to me.

5

GLITTER FROM HEAVEN

Beverly Stott had been devastated when her friend Jan had died at the age of 37 after a short and very distressing illness.

Jan had left two young children and her husband Andrew, who had gone into a deep depression and no longer wanted to live. Beverly tried everything to encourage him to get on with his life but, without the woman he had been with since he was fourteen, life no longer had any meaning.

Had it not been for the children Beverly was certain that Andrew would have ended his own life. His world had been turned upside down and he was now so unhappy that he had to force himself to climb out of bed in the morning. Beverly and her husband, Phil, kept in touch with Andrew as much as they possibly could and even invited him to their home occasionally for meals.

As the months passed by everyone was quite pleased to see that Andrew was slowly beginning to put his life back together again. He was already planning to take the children on holiday to France. Although he still missed his wife very much, the hurt was definitely beginning to ease.

After a hard day at work Beverly went to bed early on the Friday night and quickly fell into a deep sleep. She dreamt that her friend visited her to say thanks for all she had done and to tell her that she was alright. In the dream the two friends embraced and then Beverly watched tearfully as Jan bade her farewell. As she faded into the distance silver glitter cascaded down upon Beverly and at that moment she woke up. It was now morning and the sun flooded the room. It was a beautiful day and Beverly felt a sense of peace. Knowing that her friend was happy, she couldn't wait to tell Andrew about her dream.

At that moment her husband Phil appeared at the door with a cup of tea and some toast and placed the tray on the bed beside his wife. Beverly was keen to tell him about her dream but before she could speak, he said: "What's all that in your hair?" He brushed Beverly's hair with his hand and silver glitter fell onto the duvet. Beverly smiled and wiped a single tear from her eye. "Jan," she whispered. "It wasn't a dream after all."

"What is it?" asked Phil puzzled, brushing some of the glitter onto the palm of his hand. "Where did that come from?"

Beverly smiled "It's from heaven," she muttered thoughtfully. "It's glitter from heaven."

Billy says: This story is true and happened to two very dear friends of mine. I have changed their names as they requested, but the story was written word for word as they told it.

6

The Ghosts of Duke Street

In 1888 Charles Lunsdale jumped to his death from the upstairs window of 153 Duke Street. He was a businessman of high standing and well respected in the community.

All of Charles Lunsdale's business acquaintances knew him to be kind and considerate and someone who did more than his fair share in the community.

Considering that outwardly he appeared to be a happy family man and someone who was very much devoted to his wife Margaret, his death was a mystery and shocked all those who knew him.

Very soon after his death there was a rumour that his business partner had pushed him from the window after they had fought over money.

Shortly after Charles Lunsdale had died some discrepancies were in fact found when the business accounts were audited. It was this that gave rise to the suspicion that his partner had caused his death.

The mystery was never solved and since then many people have seen the ghost of a tall, well-dressed Victorian gentleman in the early hours of the morning, usually on November 12th, the day upon which Charles Lunsdale fell to his death.

Of course, the apparition could be anyone, but sightings have been reported since 1889 and were witnessed by many who knew him well.

THE GHOST OF MA BROWN

The diminutive figure of an shabbily dressed old woman has been reported shuffling her way down Duke Street, in the direction of the Monroe Public House.

Upon reaching the pub she is then seen to turn the corner at which point she disappears. The apparition is believed to be the ghost of Sally Brown, a local character who lived in nearby Henry Street somewhere around 1895.

She was a regular visitor to the Monroe Public house and was a familiar face there until the night she was brutally murdered by two young boys. Her battered body was found in Henry Street early one Sunday morning.

Although the two boys were caught and punished for the heinous crime, Ma' Brown's ghost still haunts the area. Incidentally, those who claim to have seen the old woman say that she is holding a white jug in her hands. Ma' Brown is said to have always called into the pub on a Saturday night to have her jug filled with stout. Old habits apparently die hard.

THE GHOSTLY WEDDING CARRIAGE

In the mid-twenties and thirties there were reports of a ghostly wedding carriage drawn by two horses eerily travelling along Duke Street in the direction of St Luke's Church.

Those who witnessed the spooky phenomenon said that it disappeared two hundred yards away from the junction where the traffic lights are.

The ghostly carriage is believed to be the wedding coach of Mary McNamara, a young woman whose wedding day turned to disaster when the coach in which she was travelling collided with another carriage on the way to the church.

Both she and her father were killed and the ghostly apparition of her carriage continued to be seen up until the beginning of the Second World War. In fact, it's quite interesting to note that quite a lot of ghostly manifestations disappeared completely when the war began.

Nonetheless, you would be wise to take care when walking down Duke Street in the dead of night, you never know who you'll meet!

WHERE IS JOSEPH SANDERS?

There is no doubt that Duke Street is steeped in history and has been the home to many famous people in days gone by. I have said elsewhere that Victorian physicist, Sir Oliver Lodge once had offices in Duke Street.

He had a keen interest in the phenomena of Spiritualism and devoted at least a part of his life searching for a way in which to scientifically prove that there was life beyond death.

Little known occultist, mystic and magician Joseph Sanders also lived in Duke Street some time at the turn of the 20th century. He was also a wealthy trader and was known to be ruthless in business. Because of his involvement in the occult he had very few friends and was feared by everyone who knew him.

Joseph Sanders was tall, dark and extremely handsome. He was always seen walking down Duke Street with a different lady each time. It was in fact one of his lady admirers who tried to kill him in a jealous rage.

She waited for him outside 73 Duke Street where he was then living. As he approached the front door Grace Darlwinter emerged from the shadows and shot him at point blank range, twice in the chest and finally in the forehead.

Although it was after 11pm, it was near Christmas and Duke Street was quite busy with couples wending their way home. Those who witnessed the event said that Joseph Sanders did not flinch as the shots rang out, almost as though she had fired blanks. He is said to have grinned at Grace Darlwinter then turned to disappear into the house, closing the door behind him. Although a neighbour informed the police, Joseph Sanders could not be found. In fact, when his home was searched there was nothing there at all. The rooms were absolutely empty and there were no signs at all of Joseph Sanders. He had seemingly disappeared without trace and was never, ever seen again.

Billy says: World renowned 19th century physicist Oliver Lodge once had an office in Duke Street for some years whilst he was lecturing at Liverpool University. After the death of his son Raymond, Oliver Lodge devoted a great deal of his time and efforts, not to mention his professional reputation, to scientifically proving that there was life after death – a sub-atomic existence where we go when we die.

7

THE GHOSTS OF LIVERPOOL'S PICTURE HOUSES

M any of Liverpool's picture houses have long since closed down and those that have managed to survive are struggling with progress – and sattelite television.

A couple of years ago now I went to Woolton cinema and was surprised to see no more than ten people sitting patiently for the film to begin. Gone are the days when cinemas were full to capacity and I used to queue with my parents in the pouring rain for tickets to see the latest Western or musical epic.

I used to roll about laughing in my seat as my mother sharply nudged my dad to stop him snoring. Come to think of it, my dad always fell asleep regardless of what the film was about. I never thought I would hear myself saying what my father used to say to me: "Those were the days." Nonetheless, those were the days when a trip to the pictures was the highlight of the week.

THE MAGGIE

The Magnet, or the 'Maggie' as those living in Wavertree affectionately called it, was almost an institution and the centre of the universe to all us kids, at least on a Saturday morning.

The Saturday Matinee at the Maggie meant Superman, Flash Gordon, Batman and Robin and The Lone Ranger. After this we would gallop home on our make-believe horses along the

Bishopgate Street entry, not stopping until we had reached the waste ground at Wavertree Vale for fear that the Apaches would get us. However, they never did. Our horses were always fast enough to get us home in time for tea.

The Maggie though had another more sinister side – it was haunted!

May Blenkinsop was a cleaner there in the early fifties and was often in the cinema with only her friend Joan Hughes, who was also a cleaner, for company. As they brushed the discarded ice cream wrappers and cigarette boxes along the rows of seats, neither one thought that the Maggie was haunted and that they were actually being watched.

It wasn't until May had to clean the women's toilet early Sunday morning that she came face to face with a ghost. As she busied herself with her brush she heard a shuffling sound coming from the toilet cubicle and swung round quickly to see a woman in a red coat making her way through the door into the cinema. May followed the woman but she had gone!

"What's the matter?" called the other cleaner. "You look as though you've seen a ghost."

"I think I have!" retorted May with a somewhat shocked look on her face. "Did you see someone come out of the toilet?"

"No!" came the puzzled reply. "No one!"

"Then I have seen a ghost!" May sat down on the nearest seat and nervously lit a cigarette. "I can't believe it!" she exclaimed. 'You'll have to clean the toilets. I'm not going in there again."

It wasn't until three weeks later when May's friend failed to turn up for work that May saw the lady again. She had just turned the cinema lights on and had begun to make her way down the centre aisle towards the front of the cinema.

She had forgotten all about her ghostly encounter three weeks before and was silently remarking to herself just how cold it felt. As she collected her brush and cleaning utensils from the cupboard in front of the screen, she heard a voice from behind and turned to see who it was.

She knew that the assistant manager was busying himself at the box office and thought that he had come in to speak to her. But there was no one there. She felt the hairs stand up on the back of her neck and a chill pass through her whole body.

Her eyes moved nervously across the dimly lit cinema when she caught sight of the woman in a red coat walking up the aisle away from her. May leaned her brush against the wall and began to pursue the woman but as she got close to her she just disintegrated into nothingness. May was totally spooked now and immediately decided that she'd had enough.

After listening to her protestations, the assistant manager persuaded May not to do anything too drastic and so she agreed to come in the following morning to finish the cleaning. She needed time to recover from her ordeal and at least tomorrow Joan would be back in work to keep her company.

Over the following weeks both May and Joan saw the woman in red several times. May wondered why, in all the years they had worked there, neither had seen anything ghostly before.

"You've imagined it all!" scoffed the manager when he was told. "There are no such things as ghosts!" However, his mind was quickly changed when he looked up to see the woman standing over him one Saturday night in the office.

There were many sightings of the woman in red over the years and she was eventually given the appropriate name of 'Maggie'. Although the Magnet Picture House closed some years ago it was reopened as a wine bar some time later.

I am quite sure though that the woman in red is still there somewhere, perhaps sitting at the bar, or even sitting in her favourite seat patiently waiting for the big film to begin. For many of us the Maggie will never change and will always be the place where fantasies were fulfilled on a Saturday morning.

Billy says: Since writing this story the Maggie has yet again changed from a wine bar to a roofing company and builder's storage. Such a pity!

THE RIALTO

I suppose, like many other people in Liverpool, I always knew the Rialto as the Rialto Ballroom, even though it was both a cinema and a ballroom.

My parents occasionally took me there and this was usually on a Saturday or Sunday night. I don't know whether it was just because I was young but it always seemed to be very dark when we parked the van on the waste ground at the back of the Rialto and made our way round the side to the front entrance.

As a child I felt quite safe holding on tightly to my mother's hand, even though my father would walk purposefully ahead of us, he said to buy the tickets before the big picture started. It was 1952 and I was six years old, and as long as mum and dad were with me I wasn't afraid of anything or anyone.

I remember the feeling as my little legs struggled to climb the high marble steps leading into the foyer of the cinema, suddenly being overwhelmed by the familiar smells one always associates with pictures houses.

The Rialto wasn't the most welcoming of Liverpool cinemas, but it was different and had an extremely unusual ambience.

Vera Smith was my mother's friend and a part-time cashier in the Rialto. She apparently hated working there but did so to make some extra money. She told my mother that she disliked Saturday nights and staying behind to cash up.

Apparently Saturday nights meant working late and, as the last bus from town was around 11pm, this meant she would frequently have to make her way down Upper Parliament Street alone to where she lived in Newstead Road at the top of Smithdown Road.

Although Vera was a sturdy woman used to fending for herself, she didn't relish the idea of this every Saturday night. "I'll have to find something else," she always complained to my mother. "And the bloody place puts the fear of God in me as well! The place is haunted!" She proceeded to tell my mother. "Haunted by a tall, black American soldier we call Mr Walls, because he's nearly always seen by the ice cream kiosk."

There was an American base at Burtonwood, just outside of Liverpool and the 'Yanks' as they were called frequently came into the city for a night out. 'Mr Walls' had been going out with one of the girls who had worked in the Rialto during the war. He had apparently promised to marry her after the war but had been killed when the plane he was travelling in was shot down during a bombing raid over France.

His girlfriend was devastated and had committed suicide some weeks after receiving the news. Mr Walls was frequently seen in the foyer, where he used to wait for the girl he loved, almost as though he was carrying on the same routine after his death.

The ghostly GI was also occasionally sighted standing in a door at the side of the Rialto lighting a cigarette. Eyewitnesses said that Mr Walls, the smiling soldier, simply disappeared as they passed him by.

The Rialto was sadly destroyed by fire during the Toxteth riots in the early eighties. I wonder if Mr Walls is still around, or has he now been reunited with the girl he loved and was going to marry?

GHOSTLY GOINGS ON AT THE CAMEO

On March 19th, 1949, the Cameo Cinema in Webster Road was the scene of a brutal double murder.

Assisted by his associate Bernard Catterall, cinema manager Leonard Thomas was counting the day's takings ready for the bank the following morning, when they were surprised by a masked gunman. Refusing to hand over the bag of cash the gunman shot the two men at point blank range, killing them instantly. Charles Connolly, aged 26, and 27-year-old George Kelly were arrested for the crime. However, Charles Connolly was only charged with conspiracy and being an accessory, whilst George Kelly was found guilty of murder and sentenced to death.

Kelly was executed at Walton Prison by Albert Pierrepoint and his assistant Harry Allen on March 28th 1950. Charles Connolly was released from prison in 1957 and died in 1997.

The Cameo Cinema resumed business almost immediately after the murders had taken place, but some months later sinister goings on were experienced by two of the usherettes working there. Phyllis Bradshaw twice reported to the new management that the ghostly figure of a man stood behind her moaning as though he was distressed about something. Although completely unrelated, Joan Clerk claimed to have seen one of the murdered men standing in the office doorway on three separate occasions.

Although there is no evidence that the ghostly apparitions were directly connected to the murders, the fact cannot be ignored that the murders did appear to precipitate all sorts of spooky goings on at the Cameo Cinema.

Unfortunately, the Cameo has long since gone and houses now stand in its place. I am quite certain though that the ghosts of everything that went on in the Cameo picture house over the last twenty or so years of its life are still there, somewhere in the darkness of Webster Road.

8

THE GHOST OF MARY GREY

Apart from the fact that her husband had been killed in the First World War, very little was known about Mary Grey. She lived alone in one of the smart terraced houses in Grant Avenue overlooking Wavertree Park, or the 'Mystery' as it was always affectionately known.

Mary could be seen every morning at 8am making her way through the park gates and heading in the direction of Wellington Road on the other side. She was quite sprightly for a woman of 79 and so the journey through the park probably took her no more than fifteen minutes. Mary's neighbours wondered why she was always in such a hurry and why she would always make her way through the park at the same time every morning.

Mary was a private woman and, although extremely friendly, she never seemed to have time for the usual neighbourly chit-chat.

It was November 1936 and the morning was bright and clear but chilly. As usual Mary left her home at the same time and, after checking that her front door was firmly closed, began making her way across the road in the direction of the park gates. It was there that she exchanged some pleasantries with her next door neighbour, Joe McDermott, who was taking his dog for its obligatory morning walk. He watched Mary for a few moments as she began making her way through the park.

Apart from another woman also walking her dog, the park was absolutely deserted. From that day to this no one knows exactly what happened when Mary Grey made her way alone through the park, for she was never seen again until 1938.

This time though it was Margaret Harrison who came face to face with Mary as she walked across the road in the direction of the park gates. "Good morning, Margaret," said Mary in that same cheerful voice. "Isn't it a beautiful morning?"

Margaret was somewhat taken aback and stopped in sheer amazement at seeing the unchanged Mary Grey. She stood on the pavement watching her neighbour move through the gates and make her way into the park.

Mary had disappeared without trace for two years and had reappeared as though nothing had happened. Margaret wanted to tell someone but there was no one around. She wanted to run after Mary Grey to ask her where she had been and to tell her that the Mason family now lived in her house. But as these thoughts passed quickly through her confused mind, she watched with her mouth agape as Mary disappeared into nothingness!

Margaret could not believe exactly what she was seeing and wondered whether she had imagined it all. She slowly looked down to her little dog Lilly in search of support but she simply whimpered and lowered her head to the ground. Mary Grey had gone – but not forever!

Mary Grey has been seen many times over the years, walking from her home in Grant Avenue and then heading towards the park gates on the other side of the road. On occasions she has passed the time of day to a passer-by only to then disappear into thin air without so much as a trace.

9

LIVINGSTONE DRIVE SOUTH

Workmen involved in the refurbishment of this Victorian house that was once home to a wealthy trader and his family, encountered far more than they bargained for during the course of their work.

Whilst clearing out the cellar, two young workmen heard disembodied voices echoing through the darkness. An icy chill accompanied the voices causing the young men to make a hasty retreat. "It's all your imagination!" scoffed their boss. "It was probably the sound of the wind and nothing more!" But the two workmen refused to go back into the cellar.

As the refurbishment continued the two young workmen forgot the ghostly voices in the cellar and set about their individual tasks. It was three days into the job and more tradesmen had moved in to help with the old house's transformation.

Jack Sedgely had decided to carry on working whilst the other men had broken for lunch. As he set about taking some measurements on the broad Victorian staircase, his attention was broken by the diminutive figure of an elderly lady standing on the landing at the top of the stairs. For a moment he didn't think anything of it, but just thought she had perhaps wandered in from the street to have a look around.

Jack smiled at the woman, half expecting her to say something, but she disappeared before his eyes. He nearly fell down the stairs with fright and had to steady himself by grabbing hold of the banister. "What the…" he stuttered in disbelief. "Where's she gone?"

Jack did a thorough search of the top of the house but the old woman was nowhere to be found. Although he'd never really believed in ghosts or anything to do with the paranormal, the whole experience completely unnerved him and he decided to take the rest of the day off.

The paranormal activity did not end there. On the Friday night when all the workmen had put away their tools and left for the weekend, the security guard was just about to inspect all the rooms before making the building secure when he heard muffled voices and footsteps on the stairs.

He made his way quickly to the front of the house and saw a young couple ascending the stairs. He called out to them but his voice just resounded through the empty house and he watched with amazement as the two figures disintegrated on their route to the top of the staircase. An eerie silence pervaded and, although all the doors and windows had been closed, an icy chill suddenly passed through the house. The young security guard froze to the spot and he could hear muffled voices and giggling echoing across the landing at the top of the stairs.

Although he did not scare easily, fear propelled him quickly along the hallway and through the front door, where he stood on the step trembling and trying desperately to compose himself. All the workmen were now certain that the house was haunted, but the job had to be done, even though the house itself obviously objected to the intrusion.

After my visit to the house I concluded that there were in fact several paranormal entities, none of which were menacing. However, there was one discarnate presence that caused me a little concern. This was a lady who had hanged herself at the beginning of the 20th century in one of the rooms.

However, the house has now been completely refurbished and, although this cosmetic makeover will not affect the paranormal structure of the house, it will make it much more pleasant for the future tenants.

10

MRS MARY SLATER
AND THE POLTERGEIST

The dictionary definition of a poltergeist is 'a noisy or mischievous spirit'. However, this is not always so as in 40% of poltergeist cases the phenomena is the result of a build up of energy created by the minds of the 'living' and not paranormal activity produced by the 'dead'.

The remaining 60% may be divided in to two categories: 'friendly and playful' and 'malevolent and threatening'.

Many misconceptions about poltergeists have arisen from Hollywood hype and media coverage and, although there may be the isolated case in which poltergeist phenomenon is extremely evil and violent, these are most definitely in a minority, as the majority are at worst just disruptive and mischievous. Even the most malevolent are more often than not highly exaggerated by those who experience them, and then blown out of all proportion by the media as a direct consequence.

During the course of my research I have encountered many different kinds of poltergeist phenomena and have come to the conclusion that the way in which they are perceived has a great effect upon the power and strength with which they manifest.

I am quite certain that this is the primary reason why poltergeists are often associated with puberty and children, as the embryonic psychic energy created by young children is somehow able to interact with certain so called poltergeist manifestations.

A naturally nervous child can cause poltergeist activity to

appear almost malevolent, whilst a child with a happy, relaxed and outgoing disposition often causes poltergeist activity to be quite playful, almost like 'Casper', the cartoon character.

However, before we can reach any definite conclusions about the phenomenon of the poltergeist and its numerous manifestations, it is important first of all to make a detailed analysis of what information is available to us.

For 12 years, Mrs Slater from Ormskirk believed that the spirit of her 'dead' husband was communicating with her by moving ornaments and items of furniture.

She had developed an excellent method of having conversations with him by using certain objects in the home to obtain his responses to her questions. For a 'Yes' he would rattle the coffee table in front of the television, for 'No' he would move the cushion on the settee.

Although the method she used was quite crude, for her it was sufficient to know that Ernie was around and looking after her.

This sort of phenomenon is quite familiar to anyone who has a lot of experience with paranormal activity, and the Spiritualist would probably attribute it to 'spirit' or some other discarnate source. However, in the case of grieving Mrs Slater, who wanted and needed so much to receive some sort of communication with her 'dead' husband, her desperation created an incredible mental force that attracted an extraneous supernatural power. This so-called 'power' was able to gather great strength from the force created by Mrs Slater's emotions and was therefore able to 'feedback' exactly what she expected to happen.

Unbeknown to Mrs Slater she was the architect of the whole paranormal scenario and, although there was some sort of interaction with discarnate energy, the communications were most certainly not from Ernie her 'dead' husband as she was later to find out.

When Mrs Slater was ill and in need of some support from Ernie, everything then went wrong. The fact that she was weak and extremely depleted of energy simply sufficed in precipitating the negative force of whatever it was that regularly communicated with her. When I was called to her home I was amazed to see that Mrs Slater's living room looked as though it had been devastated by a hurricane. The so-called poltergeist had revealed its true identity and this was NOT Ernie, but a build up of negative energy that had eventually culminated into an extremely fierce and almost malevolent force.

The effects of this on Mrs Slater were quite profound and although the poltergeist itself did not cause any physical harm to her, she died three months later, they said of a broken heart.

Billy says: I have always felt that the coroner's report was a classic proverbial 'cop out' and an obvious admission of not knowing what was wrong with Mary Slater. I have always believed that even when poltergeist entities do not appear to inflict any obvious physical harm, there are ways in which these extremely destructive forces can infiltrate a person's mind and thus facilitate death.

11

WHAT ARE POLTERGEISTS?

The question 'What are poltergeists?' is one that experts have endeavoured to answer for many years, seemingly without any success at all.

In fact, the poltergeist phenomenon remains one of those mysterious questions to which one single answer will not suffice. The fact is we can only offer a theoretical explanation for the whole phenomena, as each poltergeist is nearly always different from the others and cannot therefore be slotted into one compartment. Although the dictionary definition of a poltergeist is 'mischievous or noisy spirit', this only offers an explanation for the collective manifestations of the poltergeist and before any conclusions are actually drawn, a detailed analysis of each phenomenon is needed.

Furthermore, it is quite evident to me that the majority of poltergeists do not have what can be defined as 'intelligence', even though they appear to be mentally active and are very often mentally responsive.

Although some poltergeist activity is most definitely the product of a discarnate mind, these are in the minority and I would say that the majority of poltergeists are the manifestations of pockets of energy that are somehow collectively activated by an incarnate mind.

A house can quite easily take on the collective psychic characters of all those who live or have lived there over the years.

Pockets of energy made up of thought matter accumulate, quite often, in one specific area of the house and these may find an extremely powerful resonance with the psyche of one of the inhabitants. The energy appears to impinge itself upon the individual's aura and is greatly affected by his or her moods, temperament and general character. The longer that person lives in the same psychic environment, the stronger and more powerful the build-up of energy becomes. The person and the house itself are very often co-operators in the whole creation of the poltergeist phenomenon.

Generally speaking it is the whole family who provides the initial energy for the poltergeist, which is, in the majority of cases, stored in the psychic structure of the house itself. The bricks and mortar of which the house is constructed collectively manifest as a sort of psychotic structure – that is a house with two individual psychic personalities. More often than not the poltergeist draws its energy and power directly from the immense reservoir built into the psychic structure of the house. This energy is perpetuated by those who live within the confines of the house and so the poltergeist gathers strength and momentum the longer it is allowed to persist.

When a poltergeist is the manifestation of a mischievous spirit it is quite often extremely manipulative and sometimes possesses the power to infiltrate an incarnate mind. This phenomenon should not be confused with 'possession', as the person is nearly always in total control, but may find him or herself occasionally behaving completely out of character.

Even when the poltergeist is not active it is nearly always present and may exert great control over the whole atmosphere of the house. It is quite possible for the poltergeist to remain silent with no visible signs of its presence and yet to interfere with the normal everyday routine of the family and even cause unhappiness and illness.

Whilst the early stages of a poltergeist's manifestation may be quite dramatically spontaneous, in most cases it needs to build up to a crescendo and often begins simply by vibrating an object in the room. It would appear that this is done to catch someone's attention in the household and once this has been achieved it can then obtain its strength to produce even more psychokinetic activity (the movement of objects).

The occupants of the household may find that their sleep patterns are greatly disturbed as the poltergeist infiltrates the overall aura of the family.

The lack of sleep results in a lowering of each family member's resistance making him or her more susceptible to the poltergeist's influence. It is not certain however whether it does this intentionally, or whether it is simply the natural process it has to go through before it fully manifests.

It is whilst the mind is in the hypnogogic state, just before it slips into the realms of sleep, that the person is at their most vulnerable and more likely to be affected by poltergeist activity. A good night's sleep makes the mind strong and less vulnerable to discarnate influences. The victim of such an attack should therefore always ensure that at least three good night's sleep are achieved each week, even if this means staying in a friend's house or even a hotel.

Although it is not always the intention of the poltergeist to inflict physical harm, it can be extremely exhausting and deplete the human mind of energy. If there is a lot of poltergeist interaction, an occasional break is highly recommended to enable the mind to be replenished. Dealing with a poltergeist is very often just like dealing with a hyperactive child, and so one needs to be extremely disciplined and exert power over the poltergeist very early in the association.

Some poltergeists are the manifestations of dissatisfied spirits who need excitement to give them a 'buzz' and to perpetuate their existence. Overall poltergeists are not the malevolent creatures we are often led to believe by Hollywood and the world of science fiction, and I do believe that the bad press they receive is nearly always born out of ignorance and a misunderstanding.

Malevolent poltergeists do exist, but I must say these are in the minority and are extremely rare occurrences.

THE HUMAN MIND

The human mind is an incredibly powerful entity and is quite capable of creating its own demons without any intervention at all from the supernatural world.

We are in fact constantly peopling our own private portion of space by the way we think. The thoughts we create and discharge during the course of our lives are very often sent forth with such intensity that a blueprint of our own personality is gradually established in the psychic atmosphere surrounding us. In other words we create our own subtle atmosphere so therefore should be in total control at all times of the space in which we live.

We attract to ourselves the external manifestations of our own thoughts and so in some cases the poltergeists that manage to infiltrate our space do so in response to the subconscious signals we are continually sending out. There are, therefore, a minority of poltergeist manifestations that have been solely created from the accumulation of our own thought energies. Poltergeist activity may come in direct response to one's own inner feelings or thoughts and may externally represent the fears and joys of the subconscious mind. Sometimes a poltergeist can be described as a 'radio-controlled' toy and, although you may be totally unaware of it, both the poltergeist and you are co-operators in the whole scenario of the paranormal phenomena.

People often ask: "Can a poltergeist be touched?" This question has more than one answer. There are occasions when the poltergeist may feel quite solid and tangible even though it is invisible to the physical eye. In most cases even the most insensitive person may experience poltergeist activity and even physically make contact with it.

However, there are occasions when the offending force is only experienced subjectively and may only manifest within the confines of the person's mind. This phenomenon is perhaps the most terrifying, as the whole experience is similar to a psychotic illness and, if allowed to persist, may even cause the person to have a complete mental breakdown.

You should now begin to understand that the word poltergeist is most definitely an umbrella term for a broad spectrum of paranormal phenomena, as the cases are so varied and cover a fairly extensive area.

The mind is the common denominator when dealing with poltergeist activity and a poltergeist quite often takes on the personality of the mind it is endeavouring to influence. It is important therefore to eliminate fear completely when confronting any sort of evil spirit or poltergeist phenomena.

Although poltergeists are mostly invisible to the physical eye, the effect they produce is often extremely visual and leave no doubt in the mind that 'something' out of the ordinary is taking place.

Poltergeists are insidious, and once fully established in the home are able to affect all the senses. Unpleasant smells are often followed by unusual sounds, such as rumbles and even hissing.

Telekinetic activity is usually only produced once the poltergeist has fully established itself in one's life and the more interest it is able to attract the more varied the phenomena it is then able to produce. In fact, there is absolutely nothing at all that a poltergeist cannot achieve, particularly once it has got one's total interest and co-operation.

POLTERGEISTS AND CHILDREN

When discussing poltergeists one particular question always seems to arise: "What part do children play in the manifestation of poltergeists?"

It is thought that children in puberty can exert an extremely strong influence on the poltergeist phenomena, perhaps clearly indicating that hormones are able to somehow cause some sort of interaction between the invisible entity and the mind of the child.

In all my years of experience I have never witnessed any physical harm being inflicted by a poltergeist, but I have, in the past, seen a child forming an extremely close relationship with a poltergeist.

At this point I must reiterate that although malevolent poltergeists do exist, they bear no relation to those created by Hollywood and the science fiction writers' pen. In fact, there is often a close association between the phenomena of the poltergeist and the mind of a creative child. If a child possesses an active imagination, he or she is more able to subconsciously manipulate and control the activities of a poltergeist.

When children are definitely involved in the manifestation and activities of a poltergeist, it might be said that the poltergeist phenomenon itself is merely the external representation of the child's thoughts. In such cases the poltergeist phenomena usually begins to dissipate and will disappear completely once the child reaches the ages between 15 and 17 years.

To conclude though it must be said that children DO NOT always realise that they are responsible for the poltergeist's activities, as such interaction is performed at an extremely deep subconscious level.

It must also be realised that poltergeists fall into two very different categories. The first is the manifestation of a discarnate soul who simply delights in causing mayhem and havoc, albeit in a playful and mischievous way, and the second is produced by a build up of psychic energy that is often created and then precipitated by an over-active juvenile mind. The latter is far easier than the first to eradicate from the home, as with this the process of 'clearing' may be initiated simply and very quickly.

In the majority of cases the poltergeist phenomenon is greatly exaggerated and, in my 25 years plus experience as a paranormal investigator, I have found fear to exert the greatest influence when there is poltergeist activity and not the poltergeist itself.

In saying this there have been times during poltergeist investigations when I have felt almost as though my brain was about to explode or be wrenched from my skull. In one such situation I felt as though I had no control over my thought processes and that I was surely going to die.

Generally speaking though, poltergeist phenomena is at worst terrifying and at best quite fascinating.

ORBS OR SPIRIT LIGHTS

An extremely common paranormal experience is the orb or spirit light. These often appear as intense bright lights moving around a darkened room and usually appear high in the corner by the ceiling.

Spirit lights can sometimes appear in different colours and can occasionally manifest in groups gyrating simultaneously through the darkness. They nearly always seem as though they are moving in mid air, but it's not uncommon for them to suddenly appear against the wall or ceiling.

Although the majority of spirit lights are spirit manifestations, there can sometimes be an extremely natural geological explanation. Triboluminescence is a geological phenomenon created by the friction of two quartz deposits. When this phenomenon occurs below ground at a particular location it can also precipitate chemical changes in the brains of certain people, causing them to 'see' apparitions or ghostly manifestations.

LEY LINES

Another natural cause of ghostly manifestations is the phenomenon of ley lines, naturally occurring subtle channels strategically found in certain geographical locations.

Some experts believe that ley lines convey energy through the planet, and where these are found to converge, paranormal phenomena are more likely to occur.

12

The Shadow on the Stairs

David Cooper was nine years old and very intelligent for his age, but since his parents had separated six months before he had become quite withdrawn and very rarely smiled.

All the encouragement in the world could not make David play out with his friends. He had lost his father and now his biggest fear was that he would lose his mother too.

When David started having nightmares his mother thought it was time to seek professional help. David's doctor referred him to a child psychologist who, after only one consultation, concluded that he was simply in need of a lot of love and affection and that, given time, he would be alright. However, this did not solve the problem for David's mother who had been forced to watch her son change from a happy, outgoing little boy, to a sad and extremely quiet and introverted child.

David then began complaining that he was being woken up in the middle of the night by a shadowy figure standing in the corner of his room. The only way that David could get any rest at all was when his mother allowed him to sleep in her bed. She was going out of her mind with worry and his condition was getting worse. Things got so bad that she couldn't leave her son alone even for a couple of minutes. He appeared to be terrified and would cry that the shadow was going to get him. The phenomenon appeared to be stronger on the stairs and frightened David so much that he wouldn't walk up them alone.

Eventually he was admitted to Alder Hey Hospital for tests. However, it seemed that when he was taken away from his home environment he became quite rational, calm and coherent. A female psychiatrist suggested that perhaps it would be a good idea to seek the assistance of someone with knowledge of the paranormal and, in particular, someone who understood how children are affected.

David's mother contacted me two weeks before Christmas 1986, and I arranged to go and see them the following morning. They lived in Blantyre Road, off Smithdown Road. As soon as I entered the house I was overwhelmed with a feeling of foreboding and I knew right away that some unhappy event had taken place there many years before.

After meeting David I could see that he was a perfect channel for discarnate energy and was also a prime example of a young medium. He was extremely sensitive and psychically wide-open to any paranormal activity. I spent some time in the house and eventually made contact with the spirit of an old man who had lived and actually died in the house some thirty years before. The Coopers had only lived in the house for two years.

The family who lived there before them had emigrated to Australia and they had lived there for many years. The old man appeared extremely distraught and had never been able to accept the fact that he was 'dead'! After making contact with him he immediately became abusive and wanted to know what we were doing in his house.

Although I was seeing the old man subjectively, I was aware that young David was seeing him too. As the old man spoke to me David became agitated and started to cry hysterically. I could see that the old man was delighted with this and seemed to have more energy as a consequence. Something had to be done.

The separation of David's parents had somehow precipitated his psychic senses and made him more vulnerable to the supersensual atmosphere in the house. I decided that I would have to visit the Coopers' home several times before I could persuade the old man to 'move on'.

If this didn't work I was afraid that the only other alternative would be for the family to move home.

I visited the Coopers' home every day right up until Christmas. On Christmas Eve I sat alone in the downstairs front room. I found it very strange that the old man seemed to be aware that it was Christmas Eve. Usually, a discarnate who is unaware that he or she is 'dead' loses track of time and so I knew that Christmas had some special significance to him.

The longer I spent in his presence the weaker he became. I noticed that his aggression was waning and he appeared to be making every attempt to withdraw from me. He was sapping my energy and I could see a grey mist building up in the corner of the room that seemed to be acting as a sort of paranormal screen. It was like watching an old movie as the grey mist began replaying the whole scenario of the man's death. I could see that he terminated his own life by hanging himself from the stairs. At that very moment I knew that the old man was free and would not bother young David again.

David's father returned to the family home and their son appeared to settle down to a normal life. The Coopers moved from Blantyre Road five years later, and today live in a quiet road in Allerton. David Cooper grew up into a fine young man and today is a qualified doctor working in a hospital in Cornwall.

13

THE PORCELAIN FIGURE

Nora Middleton was a staunch Catholic and believed totally in the power of prayer. Entering the living room of her little two-up-two-down terrace in Callow Road, Wavertree, was like walking into a sacred shrine.

The walls were decorated with all kinds of religious artefacts, from the Pope to Jesus and the Sacred Heart. These were strategically placed around the room, overwhelming anyone who came in with a sense of peace and serenity.

Although I am not a Catholic I enjoyed visiting Nora, particularly when I was feeling a little down or even depressed. She always instilled in me the importance of prayer and I must say she was a living example of the peace prayer can bring to a distressed and lonely mind. She most definitely had a serenity about her and claimed that this only came to her through a daily routine of prayer, meditation and a deep faith in God.

I had no cause to doubt her, for although she had very little in the way of material possessions, she definitely had something that I desperately needed. Although I couldn't quite define exactly what that something was, it shone through her deep brown eyes and was carried with every word she uttered.

Nora's soft voice never failed to impress me and I always left her house feeling far better than when I had first gone in. Whenever I was feeling a little low she would always say: "Something always happens to renew your faith. Always remember that."

She had an answer for everything and seemed to know what to say and when to say it.

Nora lived alone with her sister, Alice, who also shared Nora's faith in God. Together they lived a very simple life but followed a fairly disciplined daily routine. As well as regular prayer, this routine also included two visits a day to the local church. In fact, the two sisters did almost everything together and were thought of as being quite inseparable.

When Alice passed away suddenly Nora was devastated and went into a decline. I visited her at least once a day and whenever I could I would spend a Sunday afternoon with her. Although she was a Catholic she was very interested in my work as a medium and would ask me to share my thoughts with her about the afterlife. It really came as no surprise to me when Nora passed away in her sleep, exactly two months after her sister. She seemed to lose heart in everything and could see no point in going on.

Nora and her sister had rented the house they had lived in for the past 30 years and, as she had no family, the council moved in to clear all her belongings. I was walking past her house a few weeks later and noticed that there was a skip outside the door. It was piled high with all Nora's religious artefacts and other broken items and things that could not be sold. This was an extremely sad sight to me, for as far as I was concerned all these things represented Nora's life.

I noticed a small porcelain figure of Saint Teresa discarded on top of the skip. This was one of her dearest possessions, something she had kept from when she was a child. I retrieved it from the skip and took it home with me. I cleaned it and restored its faded colour with some paint. It has been in my possession for over 20 years now, and stands on the windowledge in my office. Whenever I am feeling sorry for myself, or perhaps experiencing a little depression, I only have to touch the porcelain figure and recall Nora's profound words: "Something always happens to renew your faith." This never fails to lift the dark cloud from my mind and make me feel better.

Recently I felt as though everything was going wrong where my work was concerned and because of many disappointments, I was beginning to lose my faith.

I had just closed the computer down for the night, and drew the curtains across in front of the figure of Saint Teresa. I then placed a small but fairly heavy table in front of the window, making certain that the drop of the curtains was securely fixed against the window ledge. I hadn't done this for any reason other than to keep the surface of my office floor clear, but in doing so the porcelain figure of Saint Teresa was secured firmly on the window ledge behind the curtains.

However, I had no sooner settled down into my bed when I heard a crashing sound coming from my office. I immediately went to investigate the noise and, to my surprise I found the figure of Saint Teresa standing on the floor in the middle of the room with the table still securing the curtains against the window ledge. This strange phenomenon sent a shiver down my spine, as the porcelain figure had performed the impossible task of passing through the curtains without disturbing them in the whole uncanny process.

As I walked fully into the room I was then overwhelmed with the sweet smell of roses. These had been Nora's favourite flowers and a fragrance that always reminded me of Nora's home. I knew then that she had been responsible for this unusual phenomenon, and her wise words came once again into my mind: "Something always happens to renew your faith. Always remember that."

14

THE GHOST OF BLACKLERS

I n 1955 Olive Day worked on the toy counter in the basement of Blackers Store in Great Charlotte Street, now Wetherspoons Wine Bar.

It was three days before Christmas and the store was busier than she could remember. The grotto was as popular as ever and Olive loved to watch the queue of little excited faces patiently waiting to see Santa.

It was just after 4pm and the queue at the grotto did not seem to be getting any smaller. Olive had just been relieved so that she could take her break.

As she wended her way through the sea of faces, in the midst of all the hustle and bustle, she noticed a little boy crying and stopped to ask him why he was so distressed. She stooped in front of him and placed a comforting arm around him, only to find that her hand passed right through him. She watched with amazement as the little boy disappeared right in front of her. Olive was speechless and as there were so many people around, she was certain others must have seen the little boy disappear.

"Did you see that?" she asked a man and woman standing beside her.

"No!" was the puzzled reply.

She noticed another woman standing by her with her two little girls. "Did you see that little boy?"

But the woman shook her head. "No, what little boy?"

Olive thought she was losing her mind. It was just like the script of an Alfred Hitchcock thriller. And now she felt as though everyone was looking at her. Olive suddenly realised that her tea break was nearly over and now she had to get back to her position at the toy counter. The disappearing little boy played on her mind all that day and even when she went home she could not put the strange phenomenon from her mind. She decided not to tell her husband Ted for fear that he too would look at her strangely and think she had gone crazy.

It was on Christmas Eve and Olive had just served the last woman in what she though was going to be a never-ending queue of people. The day had been hectic and it looked as though the rush was going to continue until closing time. As there was a lull, Olive decided to have a chat with her colleague Maureen. As she looked over her friend's shoulder she saw the disappearing little boy again walking towards her counter. This time though Olive was taking no chances and wanted to make sure that her friend could see him too.

"See that little boy?" she said, interrupting the flow of conversation.

Maureen turned and then smiled. "That's my son, David," she said happily.

"Your son?"

"Yes," answered Maureen. "He's been last-minute shopping with his sister Cathy. He said he'd call in."

Deciding that perhaps she had made a mistake, Olive quickly tried to hide the puzzled look on her face.

Maureen introduced her son to Olive, remarking: "You wouldn't think he was 10, would you? He's always been small for his age."

The more Olive looked at Maureen's son, the more she was certain it was the same little boy who had disappeared in front of her a few days before. But it couldn't have been him, just a coincidence, she thought to herself as she turned to serve the next customer.

It wasn't until the Christmas festivities were over and Olive had returned to work when she learned that Maureen's son had been killed on Christmas Eve whilst shopping with his older sister. "He ran in front of a bus," said the manager. "Maureen is devastated."

Olive too was devastated and couldn't believe what she was hearing. She felt a chill pass through her whole body and wondered why she had seen the little boy a few days before he had actually died.

Olive told no one about her experience and thought it best to keep it to herself. No one would believe her anyway, she thought.

15

THE GIRL AND HER MISCHIEVOUS SPIRIT FRIENDS

Some years ago I was called to a house in Botanic Road where all sorts of frightening things were happening. The house was home to Mr and Mrs Gerrard, their 10-year-old son and daughter aged 8.

As is usual in these cases, the family wanted to know if I could 'put a stop to it all' as life was becoming intolerable for them. I stayed overnight in the house and observed the 'usual' phenomena of rappings, doors slamming and lights turning on and off. Strange fragrances and one or two rather 'unusual happenings' fascinated me particularly: taps turning on and off; the materialisation of a child's rubber ball; and the involuntary shaking of my whole body. There were times though when even I found it all a little frightening. But then I had a job to do and a responsibility to the family.

Although all this was evidently poltergeist activity, I felt there was more to it. It wasn't until I observed (clairvoyantly) two spirit presences around the house and noticed that the little girl of the house seemed to be aware of them, that I got the first inklings of what might really be happening.

In conversation with the girl I discovered that she was indeed well aware of two regular spirit visitors. She told me that one of them was a boy about the same age as herself. She didn't like him very much because, she said, he was 'strange' and 'always angry'. The second 'visitor' was a tall, elderly man who always seemed to wear black and, although the little girl didn't say so, I had the distinct impression that she was rather afraid of this man.

She told me that her two visitors always said she was 'special'. "When I think of them," she said, "the furniture moves and they tell me I'm clever."

So that was it. The little girl possessed substantial psychic powers and her two spirit visitors were using these in some way, although exactly why and to what end I did not know.

Over the next few months I visited the family regularly, helping them to understand the little girl's abilities and helping her to learn how to control them.

Eventually, she was able to block out her two 'visitors' completely, never giving them a second thought and as she managed to successfully push the culprits away, so the phenomena which had plagued the family lessened and finally stopped completely. Nothing very frightening about that, you might think. Nor is the story particularly unusual. But 18 months later the Gerrard family moved down south because of Tom Gerrard's work.

Within six months I received a request from a woman called Ann Philips to come to her house where she was experiencing some sort of paranormal disturbance. When I checked the address at the top of the letter it was the same house in Botanic Road. Whatever the Gerrards' little girl had been able to see and affect was obviously still there in the house. And the new inhabitants also had a little girl of the same age, as I was to discover, who could also 'see' the same spirit intruders. And so it went on...

16

FATHER CHRISTMAS
IS FULL OF SURPRISES

Every country has its own legends and traditions of a Father Christmas figure leaving presents for children on Christmas Eve. And although the stories that have been handed down through the ages are similar and undoubtedly based on fact, they are, I am quite certain, far removed from the original stories of Saint Nicholas and his good works.

As a child though it is a comforting thought to think that there is and always has been a Father Christmas. We can probably all remember the rush of excitement when we were children, lying in bed on Christmas Eve and trying our hardest to stay awake to catch a glimpse of Santa coming down the chimney. It never occurred to us to question how exactly such a portly figure could squeeze down the narrow space of the chimney, or visit so many children in one night. I suppose it really didn't matter as long as the result was a pillowcase full of toys at the foot of the bed on Christmas morning.

This story is true and is about a man who was planning a special Christmas for his children until misfortune unexpectedly struck.

Harry Boyle lived in Ramilies Road off Smithdown Road, Wavertree. It was 1946 and he was fortunate to be working as a joiner for the Liverpool Corporation as it was then known.

The whole country was still recovering from the war and although Harry struggled sometimes to feed and clothe his three young sons, both he and his wife, Ann, were extremely happy in their house not far from Greenbank Park.

It was a week before Christmas and Harry and Ann had spent Friday evening putting up the Christmas decorations ready for when the children got up the next morning. Harry loved Christmas and enjoyed it just as much as the children. He particularly loved Christmas Eve and the excitement playing the role of Father Christmas, tiptoeing into the children's room to fill their pillowcases with toys and sweets.

Neither Harry nor Ann relished the thought of the children bursting excitedly into their room at 5 o'clock after discovering their toys on Christmas morning. At least at Christmas they were able to forget their problems and put all memories of the war behind them.

In previous years Harry and Ann would usually have bought all the presents by now and wrapped and secreted them away at the bottom of the cupboard so their sons would not find them. But this year Harry had ordered each of his children a special present that he would collect on Christmas Eve from a store in the city centre. Michael was now seven years old and was going to be given a bicycle; David was six and wanted a scooter and a football. Little Philip was only four and was going to be given a swing and a slide.

There would of course be other little toys to fill their pillowcases and, as the war was over and Harry had a new job, it was decided that this would be the best Christmas ever.

Although Harry had secured his sons' presents with a deposit, he wanted to make quite certain that the rest was paid off before Christmas Eve. He'd already saved some money to put to his wages, and so when he got paid the day before Christmas Eve, he hurried straight into town after work.

Harry reached the shop ten minutes before closing time and excitedly explained to the shop assistant why exactly he was there. He reached into his pocket to retrieve his wallet, but to his complete and utter shock it was not there! He frantically searched all his pockets but he'd obviously lost it along the way. "I don't know what to do!" he said to the shop assistant. "I put it in my back pocket, I know I did."

"You must be mistaken," said the lady behind the counter. "Perhaps you've left it at home."

Harry didn't know what to do. It was Christmas Eve the following night and he needed the money to buy his sons' presents.

"What time are you open till on Christmas Eve?" he asked the woman anxiously.

"As it's Christmas Eve we're open quite late tomorrow," she said, "until 9 o'clock."

Harry hurried from the shop and walked back to the corporation depot where he worked, making quite certain that he followed the same route he had taken from work to the shop. He walked the whole distance with his eyes to the ground, hoping and praying that he would find his wallet lying somewhere on the pavement.

Eventually Harry made his way slowly home, wondering what on earth his wife would say, and how the kids would feel not finding any presents on Christmas morning. All the excitement had suddenly turned to numbness inside his brain and for that single moment he silently wished that Father Christmas was real.

"What will we do?" Ann asked with a worried expression. "I know my mother will give us a little, but not enough to buy the bike and other things."

"We'll manage somehow," said Harry with a sudden look of optimism. "We'll fill their Christmas pillowcases with lots of little toys. We'll buy them the big presents after Christmas."

Harry and Ann reassured each other with a hug, and agreed that nothing was going to spoil their Christmas, that this was still going to be the best Christmas ever.

Harry finished work at 4pm on Christmas Eve and made his way straight home. There was a lot to do and Ann wanted to do some last minute shopping with the little money they had managed to borrow from her parents.

The children were in bed and Harry and Ann Boyle settled down to a welcome glass of sherry. "We'll have to make sure that the fire's out before we go to bed," Ann smiled. "Father Christmas won't be able to come down the chimney."

Before going to bed the children had left a glass of milk and some mince pies on the table for Father Christmas. "He'll be hungry," Michael had said, "Particularly after travelling so far to visit so many children."

The fire was dampened and the lights were out and silence descended upon Ramilies Road.

As expected, at 5 o'clock prompt the following morning, the bedroom door sprung open and the children ran in shouting with excitement.

The couple tiredly opened their eyes and were pleased to see their sons excitedly jumping around even with the few little toys they had managed to buy them. "I told you," said Ann, "we were worrying about nothing."

However, Harry and Ann were not prepared for the sight that was to greet them downstairs.

As they walked sleepily into the living room Michael was standing proudly by his brand new two-wheeler bicycle, David was pushing himself through the kitchen door on a yellow scooter, and young Philip was about to climb to the top of his slide.

Harry and Ann stood in the doorway wide eyed in disbelief and unable to speak. Harry's eyes moved from Michael's bicycle to Philip's slide. "Who brought this lot?" he blurted. "Where…"

He was sharply interrupted when David said. "Father Christmas of course, Daddy."

"He's eaten all the mince pies and finished all the milk!" added Michael.

Harry and Ann walked across the room and sat down at the table. The mince pies had indeed been eaten and all the milk been drunk. Ann noticed a small neatly wrapped present in the centre of the table. The label on it read: "To Harry and Ann, Happy Christmas."

"What can this be?" said Ann. "Who's it from?"

She carefully undid the red ribbon and pulled the yellow paper apart to see Harry's wallet inside.

"I can't believe this!" said Harry in a low voice. "My wallet!"

Harry opened his wallet to find his money was all there.

He retrieved a small card that was attached to the wrapping paper, on which was written "From a friend."

Father Christmas never lets us down.

> Billy says: This is perhaps one of those stories that sounds too far-fetched to be true. However, I was assured that it did actually happen exactly the way I have written it. What do you think?

17

THE MAN IN THE PURPLE MASK

In 1850 the Mill Lane Area of Wavertree was much different to the Mill Lane we know today. It was much quieter and far more rural and the only traffic seen was the occasional horse-drawn carriage or cart wending its way to a nearby farm.

Although life was a lot slower then, Liverpool was growing and the surrounding land was gradually disappearing as more and more houses were built.

Robert Ashley was a successful shipping merchant and lived in a grand house in nearby Olive Lane. All that was known about him was that he had moved from Manchester two years before, and now ran one of the most successful shipping companies in the north west.

He was regarded as one of the most eligible bachelors in Wavertree and was never seen without a beautiful young woman at his side. In fact, he was the envy of all his friends who admired everything he did. Although Robert Ashley was respected by all who knew him, he was not a conceited man for all his wealth, charm and good looks and was known to have donated large sums of money to local poor houses and orphanages.

As far as the locals were concerned Robert Ashley was a decent man who contributed more than his share to the community, and was a gentleman in every sense of the word.

Little did they know that the man whom everyone admired actually lived a double and very secret life. By day he was a businessman and entrepreneur, and by night he was a highwayman and smuggler.

In fact, no one suspected that the dashing Robert Ashley was responsible for the spate of coach hold-ups that had taken place between Liverpool and Chester over a period of four years.

The infamous highwayman had become known as the Man in the Purple Mask and, although no one was ever harmed during the robberies, his charm and gentlemanly manner became his calling card and trademark.

In fact, Robert Ashley was eventually caught because he could not resist paying attention to a pretty lady during his exploits as a highwayman. He reached across to touch a young woman's cheek and was immediately identified by another woman he had once scorned. She recognised the ring on his hand and the sweet fragrance he favoured. She reported him to the authorities and he was arrested the following morning at his home in Olive Lane.

The Man in the Purple Mask was found guilty and sent to prison for five years where he died of consumption after spending only 12 months behind bars.

GHOSTLY MONKS AND THE WELL

It was once said: 'You will find ghosts wherever you look, and ghosts will surely find you.' And I am quite certain that this is very true, particularly as we are surrounded by so much history and memories of a bygone age.

Wavertree is allegedly one of the most historic districts on Merseyside and it never fails to amaze me how many ancient locations there actually are in this comparatively small village. We only seem to notice them when our attention is brought to them through the pages of a book on local history.

Wavertree was named in the Domesday Book as Wavretreu, and although it has changed considerably since those days when it consisted primarily of farms, fields and cottages, the ghosts of those far-off days still linger, perhaps just to observe.

If you take a leisurely stroll along Mill Lane, on the left-hand side of the road there are the remains of an ancient water well, reputed to be more than five hundred years old.

It is said that when Britain was ravaged by the great plague, monks from a nearby monastery actually sold the water from the well to the locals. This dishonest monastic trade was allowed to continue for some time before the locals eventually protested and took control of the well.

Although there is no evidence to support the story, one monk was allegedly killed when he objected to the peasants taking control of what had become a very viable business. For many years now there have been consistent reports of the ghostly figures of monks stood by the ancient well in the dead of night. Over the last 20 years there have been at least eight sightings of a ghostly horse and cart there, obviously still collecting water from the well.

18

THE DISAPPEARING MAN

The phenomenon of dematerialisation is for many people something that is only found in the pages of a science fiction novel. In fact, beyond the writer's imagination this phenomenon is extremely difficult for any rational thinking person to comprehend.

However, on one sunny Autumnal morning in 1953, four eyewitnesses testified that a man disappeared in front of them.

The well-dressed, middle-aged man was seen coming out of what was then Martins Bank, (and is today a doctors' surgery) on the corner of Earl Road and Smithdown Road, more or less opposite the Boundary public house.

Ethel Jones had just crossed Earl Road and was walking in the direction of the bank when she saw the man in question coming towards her. She noticed an elderly couple walking behind the man and a young woman crossing the road to her right, all of whom were in fact close enough to witness what was about to happen. When Ethel Jones was no more than five feet in front of the man he just disintegrated into thin air. Had the astounded woman witnessed this extraordinary phenomenon alone she would have found it impossible to explain. However, luckily for Ethel Jones three other people witnessed the strange and very weird scenario.

Although the phenomenon of dematerialisation does not occur everyday, from a paranormal investigator's point of view it is perhaps far more common than one might imagine. As to why the phenomenon takes place so spontaneously no one really knows. I can only reiterate the point that I have made many times before. Such apparitions are not always spirit appearances and are very often no more than the manifestations of paranormal photographic images in the psychic atmosphere.

In the case of the disappearing man the phenomenon was probably the result of a routine he more than likely habitually went through for many years. He may even have still been alive when the phenomenon was witnessed, of this there is no way of knowing. The likelihood of the disappearing apparition being the spirit presence of the man is quite slim.

Although there are innumerable cases were a so-called 'dead' person has continued with his or her daily routine purely out of habit beyond death, this is usually done only until his or her consciousness expands to the reality of their new environment.

Mostly though, apparitions such as the one that was witnessed outside Martins Bank are little more than a paranormal image in the psychic atmosphere. Such manifestations are dependent upon the light at the time, the temperature and, more importantly, the weather.

19

A GHOSTLY MEETING IN
MASON STREET, WOOLTON

If you have ever taken a casual walk through Woolton village on a quiet summer's evening, you will know exactly what I mean when I say that very little effort is needed to be mentally transported back to those days of bonneted ladies and horse-drawn coaches.

In fact, Woolton Village is steeped in history and boasts the oldest pub in Liverpool. The Coach and Horses may have been serving refreshments longer than any other hostelry on Merseyside but this does not take away the fact that this quaint little establishment, complete with its ghosts and spooky goings on, lends itself perfectly to the whole ambience of Woolton Village. How many of those who make their way hastily to Sainsbury's during a busy lunchtime, actually realise that the little old lady who has just passed by is not real at all, but a ghost?

It was just after 4.30pm on one bleak November day in 1985 and Pat Skinner had just crossed Woolton Street and had begun walking up the slight incline of Mason Street where she had parked her car.

As she reached Woolton Cinema she noticed an old woman standing a few feet in front of her smiling. Not wanting to appear discourteous, Pat smiled back at the woman who then walked right up to face her. "Buy a lucky charm or some lucky heather?" muttered the old woman through thin lips.

Pat sighed and thought: "I might have known!" She made it a rule never to buy anything from gypsies and most certainly not on the street. The old woman was persistent though and thrust a fist full of heather under Pat's nose. "Please buy a charm or some lucky heather?" she mumbled again, her thin pale lips revealing yellow stained teeth.

Pat felt a sudden rush of anger and did not like this sort of intimidation at all. Just as she was about to give the woman a piece of her mind, the old gypsy said: "Frank will find a job in January! January 18th will be a turning point for you!"

Pat's mouth fell open. How did the old woman know that Frank was her husband, let alone that he was looking for work? Before she had a chance to respond the old woman said: "You'll have to move house mind!"

Pat felt the hairs on the back of her neck stand up and a cold shiver all over her body. "But how do you...?" she stuttered incoherently, unable to get her words out.

The old woman grinned. "You'll be alright," she muttered. "Next year will bring those long overdue changes!"

Pat still could not speak. She fumbled clumsily to retrieve her purse from her handbag and listened intently in case the old woman uttered any more prophetic statements.

The old woman eyed Pat curiously and then handed her a lucky charm and a piece of heather. Pat gave the old woman all her loose change her eyes fixed onto the gypsy's lined face. Not another word was spoken. The old woman turned and walked down Mason Street in the direction of Woolton Street then disappeared around the corner. Pat stood there for a moment then suddenly decided to pursue the old woman. When she reached the corner the old gypsy was nowhere in sight – she had disappeared completely.

Pat stood there for a few moments lost in thought. She had no idea where the old woman had come from or where she had gone, but felt somehow reassured about her personal situation. Nobody knew that Frank had been made redundant and that they had been thinking of moving. The old woman knew everything.

Pat smiled and reached into her bag to retrieve the lucky charm and piece of heather but it was not there! She searched her bag thoroughly but there was no sign of the lucky heather or the charm. Pat felt a shiver pass through her body. Thinking it was time to make her way home, she pulled up her collar to shield her face from the sharp wind that had suddenly started to blow down Mason Street, then continued her journey towards her car not more than two minutes away.

By the time Pat had pulled up outside her front door, she had already decided not to tell Frank about the old gypsy woman. He would have dismissed the whole thing anyway and laughed at her for being so silly. Besides, she wasn't so sure now that the whole thing had actually happened at all. Inwardly she prayed that it had and that the old woman's predictions would prove to be accurate.

As always, the Skinner family did not allow anything to spoil their Christmas and were now ready to face the New Year.

It was January the 18th and Bob Latham, Frank's oldest friend, telephoned from London. "There's a vacancy for someone with your qualifications," he said excitedly down the phone. "There's a house with the job. I've spoken to the boss and the job's yours, if you want it?"

Pat couldn't believe it. Everything the old woman had said had come true. She checked the date on the calendar just to make sure that it was January 18th. She smiled to herself and silently wished that she had told Frank about meeting the old gypsy woman. At least now she knew that the chance meeting in Mason Street did really happen and it wasn't a figment of her imagination after all.

20

THE LADY OF THE LAKE

Ron Lynch's daily walks with his five-year-old Labrador, Jess, had become a most needed ritual since his heart attack three years ago.

His wife Ann occasionally accompanied him, especially when the weather was nice, but on this particular bitter December morning Ron and Jess made their way across Sefton Park alone. It was just after 8am and daylight was beginning to break across the frost-covered park.

As Ron and Jess reached the grassy incline leading to the lake Ron noticed a bright glow moving slowly across the ice-covered surface. Jess became quite agitated and began to whimper, and Ron felt a sudden chill pass right through him.

There was no one else around and Ron felt slightly uncomfortable. The glow suddenly stopped moving and now from where Ron stood he could see that the bright light was in fact the figure of a young woman. Jess became even more agitated and began to pull on her lead and Ron placed a reassuring hand on her head and calmed her down.

The phantom eventually faded into nothingness, leaving Ron feeling somewhat confused by the whole experience. He stood for a few moments playing the last fifteen minutes over and over in his mind, wondering what it was all about. Deciding to make his way back home, Ron gently patted Jess and offered her his apologies, before turning to climb the grassy slope leading from the lake. He wondered whether Ann would believe his story, and couldn't wait to get home and tell her.

The following morning Ron was amazed to hear on the local radio station that the body of a young woman had been found floating on the lake, in exactly the same spot where he had seen the apparition. He felt a cold chill pass through his body and was suddenly overwhelmed with a feeling of complete and utter sadness for the young woman.

He'd never had such an experience before and most certainly did not in any way believe in ghosts or the supernatural. However, he had witnessed it with his own eyes and quietly hoped that it was an experience he would never have again.

21

LITTLE TOMMY REMEMBERS...

After five disappointing years of trying to conceive, Lyn Fairfax joyfully announced to her husband, Tom, that she was pregnant.

They were so happy and couldn't wait to tell Tom's parents and her mother, who now lived alone after the death of her father 12 months before.

Six years later, their five-year-old son, Tommy, had just started school. Because he was not a 'rough-and-tumble' child, Lyn found herself being very protective towards him. He was extremely sensitive and showed no interest in football or any of the sporting activities which other children his age participated in.

Because of Lyn's tuition, Tommy could read exceptionally well and would spend most of his time with his head buried in a book. He appeared very advanced for his age, and would often come out with the most profound statements, mystifying his parents, who wondered where on earth their little boy had come from.

After collecting Tommy from school one blustery and very cold Friday afternoon, Lyn made her way to the cleaners in Woolton Village to pick up Tom's suit and her winter coat. As she helped her son from the car, he blurted: "Where's Mason's bakery gone?"

Lyn stopped and looked at Tommy with a puzzled look. She thought she had misheard him and so asked him to repeat what he had said.

"Where's Mason's bakery gone?"

Mason's bakery had in fact gone before her son had been born, and so Lyn had wondered why he had said it. "How do you know Mason's bakery?" she asked him. "You weren't even born!"

A broad smile dawned across Tommy's lips, and he gave his mother a knowing look. "I'm your dad!" he pronounced. "Of course I remember Mason's."

Lyn felt a cold shiver pass through her body as she gazed at her son's little face. She could see he was very serious and knew that he was far too young to be playing games.

Before Lyn could utter another word, Tommy took his mother's hand and grinned cheekily. "Come on, Babs," he said quietly, "we'll have to buy our chocolate fairy cakes somewhere else."

Lyn's eyes widened in disbelief. Her son could not have known that her father called her Babs right up until the day he died. And he always bought her chocolate fairy cakes on the way home from school.

Billy says: This is a classic case of reincarnation, where a child has perfect recall of a previous life. Although quite incredible, this phenomenon is far more common that you might imagine. Many children have memories of previous lives, but unfortunately these memories nearly always fade as they get older. Some researchers into the subject have suggested that such recall is the result of genetic memory. I have personally interviewed several children, who said that they can remember living here before in another time. I must say I was convinced.

22

I Just Called To Say I Love You

Steve and David Stourton were devastated when their mother, Pat, was diagnosed with cancer. The death of their father four years before had made the family very close and now they were going to lose their mother to the same disease.

Pat did not want to die but she was quite philosophical about the whole horrible thing. Once she had put all her affairs in order, she made it clear to her sons exactly what she wanted – to be allowed to die with dignity at home.

Pat had spent most of her life as a nurse and so she knew more or less what to expect when the end came. Her only concern was that her boys would be alright when she had gone and just prayed that they would be strong enough to cope when she became too poorly to function.

Whilst Steve was the eldest at 20, 19-year-old David was far more mature and never really showed his feelings. Steve was her main concern, and Pat hoped that they would help each other through the distressing ordeal.

Although she had been given six months to live, she fell into a decline within four months and became so ill that she was unable to get out of bed. Her two devoted sons made her as comfortable as possible and even installed an intercom telephone system to make her last days a little easier for her.

Pat passed away peacefully early one Sunday morning, and although her death was expected, Steve and David were devastated. Two weeks after the funeral, Steve and David were in the living room sorting through some of their mother's papers when they heard the intercom buzzer resound through the dining room. They both froze to the spot and stared at each other.

Although it was still in place, the intercom system had been disconnected from its power source shortly after Pat had died. Thinking they had imagined it all, they dismissed the sound of the intercom and continued to sort through their mother's papers.

The buzzer sounded again, only this time with more urgency. Staring anxiously at his brother, Steve reluctantly went into the dining room where the intercom sat on the table by the window. The buzzer resounded once again, and he quickly lifted the receiver to his ear. His heart missed a beat as he heard his mother's voice say: "I love you both."

The phone then went silent. Steve felt numb and knew that his brother wouldn't believe him, and so decided not to say anything. He felt a warmth inside and was reassured about his mother, and now knew that she was alright. "What was it?" asked David walking into the room, staring curiously at his brother. "What happened?"

Steve just grinned and shook his head. "The system somehow maintained some of its power." He said quickly without thinking. "That's all."

"Spooky though?" retorted his brother. "For one moment..."

"Yes, I know." Dave interrupted. "Me too."

The truth was their mother had called to tell her boys that she was alright and that she loved them.

Billy says: I had known Pat for over 10 years, and although she believed in an afterlife, her sons did not. In fact, they were both extremely sceptical.

23

The Ghost of Quiggins

Although Quiggins in the city centre has now fallen beneath the mighty hand of progress and so-called regeneration, I am quite certain that its ghosts will not be moved and will thus linger for many years to come in the shadows of School Lane.

I met Jimmy Lindeman over fifteen years ago through our mutual fascination with memorabilia and all things connected to the past. Jimmy would collect and sell anything and everything from his little stall in Quiggins on School Lane, but I first met him when he ran the Emporium on Picton Road, Wavertree.

I wandered into his little shop to enquire about some Dinky cars and lead soldiers and found him an extremely interesting man to talk to. Apart from being quite eccentric, Jimmy Lindeman is a mine of information, level headed and down-to-earth.

It was 1990 and Quiggins was something of a shopping innovation; entering it was like stepping back into the 1960s. Practically anything could be bought in the small shops and stalls there; from clothes and furniture, to eastern jewellery and collectable records. It was an ideal location for Jimmy's emporium and he was extremely excited at the prospect of setting up his business there.

Although Quiggins then closed at 6pm precisely, the building had its own security guard and so store holders would frequently remain in the building preparing their stock for the following day. With so many collectables, the security made Jimmy Lindeman feel quite reassured.

It was two weeks before Christmas and the security guard knew Jimmy Lindeman had stayed behind to catalogue some old postcards. A potential customer was coming in the following day, so the collection had to be brought up to scratch. Jimmy was very proud of his postcards and worked meticulously until just after 9.30pm, when fatigue finally got the better of him. He secured the door of his unit and trudged the maze of shops and units towards the security guard's room. When it was empty, it could be quite eerie and, together with the pungent fragrances of sandalwood and patchouli, there was also another indefinable fragrance which always sent shivers down Jimmy's spine.

As he reached the bottom of the stairs, he noticed a woman walking towards him. It was only when she had passed him by that it occurred to him that he and the security guard were supposed to be the only ones left in the building. He immediately stopped and looked back, but she had vanished. Just in case she had been locked in the building by mistake, Jimmy alerted the security guard and together they searched for the woman.

"She went upstairs," Jimmy told the guard, "she seemed to know exactly where she was going."

"But there's absolutely nothing upstairs," the guard replied. "It's all locked up, and anyway, it's not in use."

Jimmy was obviously concerned so, to put his mind at rest, the security guard decided to take a look. They climbed the stairs to the upper floors of the building but, just as he had said, it was derelict, very dark and dismal and all locked up. There was absolutely no sign of the woman anywhere in the building. She had disappeared without trace.

The same woman appeared again on numerous occasions to other unit holders who had stayed behind to work after hours. They each described a similar series of events and affirmed that she appeared to know exactly where she was heading as she climbed the stairs and that subsequent searches, no matter how thorough, revealed that she had disappeared without trace.

The woman was not the only apparition to have been seen in Quiggins. In fact, there were numerous sightings of ghostly figures roaming through various unused parts of the old building and who disappeared into nothingness.

Billy says: Now that Quiggins has gone, where will they go to? Or will they remain in School Lane? Who knows, they may even follow you home...

24

Frog Lane: The Ghosts of Whitechapel

It is perhaps difficult for some people to believe that the Liverpool we now know and love bears no resemblance whatsoever to the Liverpool of three centuries ago.

Apart from the obvious structural differences, three hundred years ago the city was probably much less tolerant and far more aggressive, not to mention much more rural. It was then a thriving seaport and one of the fastest growing towns in the world.

Walking through the hustle and bustle of Whitechapel on a Saturday afternoon, our thoughts are usually focused primarily upon negotiating a route through the never-ending crowds, and most certainly not on the individual faces that pass us by. Most people dread the very thought of making their way through the bustling throngs of people in the city centre and we usually approach the whole ritual of shopping in an almost mechanical way, completely oblivious to our surroundings.

How then does one know whether or not one of those anonymous faces belongs to someone living or someone long since dead? I have said before that ghosts can appear to be quite solid and substantial, and very often far from the stereotypical nebulous phantoms we are led to expect.

Only a few hundred years ago, Whitechapel was the location of a dock entrance and was called Frog Lane. It was here that duels were said to have occasionally been fought. In an effort to defend the honour of his lady, a certain Thomas Knight, a young barrister, challenged a trader by the name of Ned Garrick to a duel. The young Ned Garrick was known to be an unsavoury rogue, with no intention of taking a chance on being killed by the dashing Thomas Knight.

The two men arranged to meet at the crack of dawn, halfway down Frog Lane, opposite the place where Stanley Street is situated today. Unbeknown to Thomas Knight, who was only accompanied by his second, Ned Garrick had brought along three other thugs, with the sole intention of murdering Thomas Knight.

Unfortunately for Ned Garrick, two of his companions recognised Thomas Knight as the man who had prevented them from being sent to prison. Not wanting to cause him harm, they fled quickly from the scene.

Ned Garrick was wounded in the duel, but shot Thomas Knight in the back as he walked away from Frog Lane. He was duly executed for his crime some weeks later. However, the ghosts of both the duellers are believed to still haunt the Whitechapel area in the early hours of November mornings.

In fact, numerous ghostly forms have been witnessed in Whitechapel over the years. However, the number of sightings seems to have lessened somewhat since the 1960s. It is my belief that this decrease in paranormal activity is primarily the result of a dramatic change in the social life of the city. More electro-magnetic activity has been produced as a result of increase in late night revellers in the city centre. Over the years more and more people have begun to stay up into the early hours of the morning, thus creating more activity in the psychic atmosphere and making it more difficult for apparitions to actually manifest themselves.

Once upon a time the haunting hour was believed to be around midnight, as, by then, most people were tucked up in their beds, fast asleep, with very little electro-magnetic activity in the atmosphere. Today television and radio programmes are broadcast all through the night and so ghosts have great difficulty in going about their business of frightening people!

25

THE GHOSTS OF OLDFIELD FARM

Four years ago my wife, Dolly, and I rented a farmhouse in Lower Heswall, over looking the very picturesque Dee Estuary. Waking up in the morning to such a beautiful view was so invigorating and made so much difference to each day that we never wanted to move.

There had been a dwelling house on the farm since the twelfth century and the whole area was steeped in history, from the invasion of the Vikings to the occupation of the Romans. From our window we could see the Welsh hills across the estuary, and even an approaching storm would look breathtaking as it moved menacingly across the water towards us like a dark cloud of locusts moving in to devour everything in its path.

In fact, living on the farm was an inspiration to me and we both loved being there. Just watching the sun set on the estuary was a sight to behold, and then the morning sounds of birdsong and the cacophony of cows and hens waking to the day made the whole thing just perfect (the smells were a different story!).

However, when darkness descended it always seemed to me as though a command had been given for all the creatures of the farm to lay their sleepy heads and be silent and, apart from the occasional hoot of an owl from its nearby watching place, everything was stilled beneath the dark mantle of eerie silence.

We'd been living there for five months and already spooky things had begun to happen. Strange luminous mists would move slowly about the bedroom, and disembodied whispers would echo through the night. Although I am used to such spooky goings on, I must admit that I was beginning to feel unnerved by all the phenomena that seemed to be completely out of my control.

There was a sandstone wall and cobbles all around the house, and even the slightest movement outside would resound through the empty spaces across the farm.

It was late October and the moon was hiding behind misty clouds as the hypnotic sound of the old clock in the bedroom carefully marked out each second to the hour of 1am. I was lying there unable to sleep, my mind playing over the events of the day and the things I had to do in the morning, when I heard footsteps on the cobbles outside.

I woke Dolly and together we peered nervously through the bedroom window into the darkness. By then the moon was peeping slyly from behind the misty clouds, its ghostly light dissipating the shadows across the cobbled courtyard. We gasped as we caught sight of five hooded shadowy figures, their ghostly forms silhouetted by the light of the moon as they moved purposefully off into the darkness.

We waited at the window to see the shadowy forms return ten minutes later, making their way back towards the estuary. This time we could see that they were attired in the robes of monks and were all extremely tall and walked with their heads bowed.

The following night we saw them again, and watched with intrigue as the ghostly monastic figures followed the same route across the cobbled courtyard and then returned ten minutes later to make their way back towards the estuary from whence they came. In fact, we saw the ghostly shadowy forms every night for the following two weeks and so decided to take a closer look.

On the Friday night we took a duvet and some pillows out to the car and then made ourselves comfortable ready for our ghostly encounter. To make the evening more enjoyable we took a bottle of Veuve Clicquot champagne, two glasses and armed ourselves with the appropriate paranormal equipment, an EMF meter (Electro-Magnetic Frequency) a non-contact thermometer with a laser and a night vision camera. We were all set and waited patiently for the haunting hour to approach. We sipped our champagne and glared through the car window into the darkness nervously waiting for our ghostly friends to arrive.

Unfortunately that's all we remember. We both woke up at about 4am shivering with the cold and me having spilled a glass of champagne all over my shirt. We were absolutely freezing and missed the whole spooky scenario. The following day we laughed at the thought of the ghostly figures peering at us, bewildered and wondering exactly why we were asleep in the car.

After Vikings invaded various parts of Britain, they apparently settled in and around the area of Heswall, establishing an encampment and cultivating the land. At night the whole area of Lower Heswall possesses an eerie atmosphere and it does not require much imagination to be transported back through time to when the Vikings invaded our shores. Although several hundreds of years ago there was a monastery in Dawpool, half a mile from Oldfield Farm where we lived, I still can't understand why the ghostly monks appeared where they did!

THE SINGING PHANTOM

Since we saw the ghostly apparitions on the farm we have witnessed other very spooky phenomena late at night on the marshy banks of the Dee Estuary.

My wife and I decided to take a midnight stroll down to Caldy steps, as it is called. By day it is an extremely picturesque beach right on the Dee Estuary. But in the dead of night it was a completely different story. Then, the imagination takes over.

Although pitch black, it was our intention to see if it really was as haunted as people had said. And so, holding hands firmly, we nervously descended the steps through the darkness towards the beach below.

There was only the sound of the wind and the soothing wash of the tide moving rhythmically in and out over the rocks and sand.

There was an icy chill in the air and I felt quite uncomfortable. I made a feeble excuse in an attempt to persuade Dolly to return home but, as she is much braver than me, this fell on deaf ears.

We had walked some distance down the beach and as close to the marshy banks as was safe to do so, when my wife squeezed my hand and gestured ahead in the darkness. Even though my eyesight is not too good, I could distinguish the glowing form of an old woman walking from the safety of the estuary bank towards the dark murky water.

We could both hear the old woman singing to herself as she moved further and further away from safety of the shore. This iridescent figure with a luminous glow did not look once in our direction. She eventually disappeared into the nothingness, leaving us spellbound in the freezing cold.

The apparition was not something I alone was able to see because of my mediumistic skill; we both witnessed the ghostly figure moving into the darkness of the Dee Estuary.

Although her identity is unknown, I have spoken to a few people in the area who confirmed that the 'singing lady' as she is affectionately called, is a well known ghostly figure, just as we had suspected. One elderly person told us that the singing lady lived in a cottage on the estuary over a hundred years ago and is thought to have drowned whilst trying to save her little dog.

26

THE LADY OF LIGHT

My childhood was peppered with all different kinds of psychic occurrences. Although many of them were dismissed as having no great significance, others were too remarkable to disregard and will always stand out in my mind as being integral parts of my personal spiritual development.

One such memorable event I always think of as my first real mystical experience I call 'The Lady of Light,' as that's exactly what it was.

I was about nine years old and I was playing in the front room of my house – the 'parlour' as it was known. It was a cold winter's evening and the wind was howling down the chimney, an ideal night for playing ghosts and frightening my friend Tommy Edgar.

I was turning the light on and off and making frightening spooky sounds and my friend was doing the same. All of a sudden the light refused to go back on and there was a sharp popping sound coming from the wall above the antique cabinet my father had bought at an auction some months before.

As Tommy and I peered through the darkness towards the cabinet, a faint light appeared against the wall. At first the light was quite dim but then became brighter and more intense. As we nervously watched it, not knowing at that point what to do, the light grew and metamorphosed into the shape of a lady with long robes. At this point Tommy began to cry and made a dash across the room, pulling frantically at the door handle until the door finally swung open and he was free to make a hasty retreat. I stood mesmerised by the ghostly apparition that now looked like Our Lady. It became animated and looked just like a projected image onto the wall. Gradually, though, the image became three dimensional and I could distinguish the lady's gentle features.

I ran from the room to fetch my mother, father and aunt. "Come quickly!" I called excitedly. "Our Lady is next door." I recall the look on my mother's face as she came with my aunt to investigate. My father, however, being the sceptic he was, remained in his armchair with his feet on the stool, completely disinterested in what was taking place in the adjacent room.

My mother and Aunt Sadie stood in front of the apparition ashen faced and speechless. My mother immediately decided that if I touched it I would be cured of the disease with which I suffered since I was three. She moved a chair over to the cabinet and made me stand on it. "Reach out and touch it," she said quietly, holding the chair with one hand and steadying me with the other. I reached out but before my hand made contact with it there was another popping sound and the apparition disappeared and the room fell into darkness.

Almost simultaneously the light came on in the room. My mother and Aunt Sadie stood there staring at the wall in silence. "What's happened?" I asked, somewhat confused. "Where has the lady gone?"

My mother noticed a film of iridescent pink powder all across the surface of the old cabinet. Thinking that it had some connection with the apparition, she carefully collected it into an empty pill bottle. The following afternoon a neighbour brought two nuns from the local catholic church pray in the room where the apparition had appeared.

My mother retrieved the pill bottle to show them the pink powder, but to her amazement it had completely disappeared without trace.

The nuns prayed in the parlour for nearly an hour, and then warmly told my mother we had been quite fortunate. "This was a very special Mother coming to tell a mother that everything would be alright," was one of the nun's explanations. "You have been very blessed."

Although my mother was obviously comforted by the apparition, it did seem to precede a sequent of unhappy events. A few weeks later I had lobar pneumonia and, as a result of my brother leaving home, my mother was very ill. In fact, the apparition seemed to be some sort of omen and for the months that followed our family went through an extremely unhappy period. Nonetheless, this was probably the most significant paranormal experience I have ever had in my whole life. The nuns believed that the apparition was Our Lady, but to me she was 'The Lady of Light'.

27

THE VANISHING COUPLE

Most paranormal happenings occur when you are least expecting them. In fact, if you watch for them, they very rarely happen.

People often say to me: "I've never seen anything." However, the truth is how do they know? A paranormal experience can be so spontaneous, that nine times out of ten we don't even notice it. For an example, in parapsychology there is a phenomenon often referred to as the 'corner of the eye' syndrome. This is when we are sitting down relaxing in our home alone, perhaps completely oblivious to anything but the article we are reading in the evening newspaper, when suddenly we see something out of the corner of our eye. Of course, when we swing round to look it is not there. This phenomenon is far more common than we might imagine, and one that is frequently dismissed as either tiredness or a trick of light.

In my experience as an investigative medium I have found that ghosts can appear to be quite solid and substantial and may even be quite warm to the touch.

This is an account of something which happened several years ago to an elderly couple returning from their son's wedding anniversary in Southport.

On this particular winter's night in the torrential rain, Derek and Barbara McConlon were driving along the Formby bypass towards Liverpool, when they came across a young couple, looking quite cold and drenched, standing miserably at the side of the road trying to hitch a lift. Normally 70-year-old Derek wouldn't dream of stopping for anyone, particularly so late at night, but Barbara was very persuasive and argued that they looked like nice people and it would be a kind gesture to give them a lift on such a cold and wet night.

So, reluctantly, Derek pulled into the side of the road and the couple clambered gratefully into the back of the warm car. They thanked Derek and Barbara profusely and immediately gave their names as Tricia and Dave Edgerton. It was 1969 and the couple said that they had been to a wedding in Southport and that they had missed the last train back to Liverpool.

By the time they had reached the end of the bypass, on the approach to Ince Blundell, the polite conversation between the four of them had been exhausted and a rather embarrassed silence had descended upon the car. As they were driving through Ince Blundell, Derek coughed and then asked: "Where can I drop you off?"

His question met with total silence, and so thinking that they had fallen asleep he glanced in the rear view mirror upon which he slammed on the brakes and the car screeched to a juddering halt.

"What's the matter?" gasped Barbara, grabbing the dashboard in alarm. She had been dozing for the last ten minutes or so and had been jolted awake by the sudden braking movement. She looked across at Derek and was immediately struck by his shocked expression. She turned her head to see what he was looking at through the mirror.

"They've gone!" he stammered in disbelief. "My God! Where are they?"

Barbara immediately climbed out of the car to look back along the road but it was completely deserted.

"I can't understand it!" exclaimed Derek. "They couldn't possibly have jumped out of the car. I was going much too fast. But where the bloody hell are they?"

The incident left the couple more than a little mystified and extremely unnerved. They did not know what to think and decided that the whole episode was best forgotten, at least until the following day. By morning their minds would be more or less rested and they would be better able to make sense of the unusual affair.

The following day was Sunday and Derek was enjoying his usual lie-in when Barbara suddenly came dashing into the bedroom and spread the morning newspapers on the duvet in front of Derek.

"Look at this!" she said, shaking him awake. "Look at this picture and read the story."

Derek tiredly rubbed his eyes and, suddenly noticing Barbara's shocked expression, looked at the newspaper and read the headline: NEWLY MARRIED COUPLE, TRICIA AND DAVE EGERTON, KILLED ON THEIR WEDDING DAY IN TRAGIC ACCIDENT.

28

THE MYSTERIOUS PHONE CALLS

Brenda Gibson had lived in Newhouse Road, Wavertree for eight years and had decided that it was time to make a few changes to her life.

She had been divorced for two years and although her ex-husband, Ron, still called to see the children and had often intimated that he would very much like to be involved with her again, she had no plans of ever returning to him.

"Never go back!" her mother had always advised her as a general matter of principle. "Always look forward."

And that was exactly what Brenda intended to do.

She had been to the estate agents in Allerton Road to find out what sort of prices the houses were fetching in the area and had immediately taken the decision to sell up and move to Southport, where she had always wanted to live. Now that she was in a much better financial situation, she just knew that the time was right for her to make a new start.

On the Friday afternoon, after the children had gone back to school, Brenda had decided to catch the bus into town to treat herself to a new coat and shoes. She was just about to leave the house, when the telephone rang. The caller asked to speak to someone called Jean and when she told him that he must have the wrong number, he became abusive and then hung up.

Although the call had unnerved Brenda somewhat, she quickly put it from her mind and made her way towards Picton Road to catch the bus into town. On her return, she had just put the key in the lock when she heard the telephone ringing again. She deposited her shopping on the floor in the hallway and quickly rushed to answer it.

"Where have you been?" demanded the voice at the other end of the line. "I've been trying to get you all afternoon."

It was the same man who had been abusive earlier and Brenda felt a rush of fear, which caused her heart to beat faster.

"Who is this?" she snapped, desperately trying not to appear afraid. "I have told you, no one called Jean lives here. If you ring again, I'll have to call the police."

The man became abusive once more and even addressed her by her name. He also appeared to know that she was divorced and that she lived alone with her daughters. Brenda quickly hung up on him. She could feel herself shaking and did not know what to do next. As she stood by the telephone, trying to decide whether or not to call the police, it began to ring again. She allowed it to keep on ringing for some time without answering it, but the persistent noise eventually prompted her to pick up the receiver. At first she did not speak and simply listened. She could hear someone breathing at the other end of the line and some of her fear was replaced by a sudden rush of anger.

"I've just phoned the police!" she shouted down the phone, half expecting him to hang up.

"No you haven't!" he coolly replied, with an arrogant, sneering tone to his voice. "You haven't phoned anyone. You'd better take care, living alone with your two lovely little daughters."

"You're a pervert!" she screamed, slamming down the phone.

The telephone calls had left her emotionally drained and she decided almost immediately, to carry out her threat and call the police.

It took the police some time to respond to her complaint, but eventually a policewoman called at the house the following afternoon. Although she took down all the details of the anonymous calls, Brenda noticed that she seemed completely uninterested in the incidents and appeared to be only half taking notice of what she was saying. So she expressed her deep concern and stressed that she desperately wanted something to be done about it.

The abusive telephone calls came every day at the same time and, on each occasion, Brenda reported them to the police without any satisfaction. Eventually, she called into Lawrence Road police station to lodge a formal complaint. She filled in a statement there and then and was assured that something would be done, and she had no sooner returned home, than the duty sergeant at the police station rang her.

"We are putting a trace on all your calls," he assured her. "There's no guarantee that we'll catch the caller, but at least it might deter him."

Satisfied that the police were now going to do something about the problem, Brenda breathed a sigh of relief and sat down with a nice cup of tea and a digestive biscuit, feeling more relaxed than she had since the calls had begun.

But, no sooner had she settled down in her chair, than the anonymous menace telephoned again.

"You shouldn't have gone to the police," he hissed, threateningly. "You're a naughty girl and naughty girls get punished."

Brenda knew that she had to keep him talking so that the police would have enough time to trace the number that he was calling from.

"How do you know I've been to the police?" she asked, her voice shaking nervously, "or are you just surmising?"

"I know everything about you," he continued. "You're also thinking about moving to Southport."

Brenda froze. She hadn't even told her daughters about her intention to move to Southport and wondered how on earth he could know so many details about her life.

"I don't know what you're talking about," she bluffed. "I wouldn't dream of leaving Liverpool."

"You're right!" he hissed, "You won't be going anywhere." He began to sound even more aggressive and almost manic.

"I'm going to pay you and your daughters a visit soon!"

At that point the line went dead. No more than thirty minutes later, two policemen called to see Brenda.

"Did you manage to trace the number?" she asked eagerly. "Have you caught him?"

They followed her into the living room and suggested that she should sit down. They looked quite serious and were glancing nervously at each other, as though in search of moral support for the task which lay ahead.

"How long have you lived here, Mrs Gibson?" asked one of the policemen.

"Why?" she asked, curiously, her eyes moving from one to the other. "What's that got to do with the phone calls?"

"How long, Mrs Gibson?" he insisted, a note of urgency in his voice.

"Eight years," she answered. "But why?"

The policeman who was speaking looked at his colleague with a somewhat puzzled expression on his face. The other police officer then continued the explanation.

"I really don't know how to tell you this." He paused, and then glanced uncomfortably at his associate. "We traced the number to this address." He watched Brenda for a response. "It was traced to your own number."

"What?" she retorted. "It's not possible. I've only got one phone."

"We know," continued the policeman, "We checked our records and Alan McCarthy lived here fifteen years ago. He was cautioned several times by the police for making obscene phone calls to a middle-aged lady in Speke." He paused, and lowered his eyes uncomfortably. "In fact, he murdered her."

"Oh my God!" Brenda gasped. "And he's obviously out of prison now. I hope you're going to arrest him before he does any harm to my children?"

The two policemen looked at each other, and then turned towards her. There was a moment's silence before one of them spoke.

"That won't be possible, Mrs Gibson," he said solemnly.

"You see, Alan McCarthy is dead! He committed suicide shortly after he had killed the woman in Speke."

"I don't understand!" she stuttered. "But how…"

"We don't understand it either, Mrs Gibson," interjected the policeman, who was now smiling. "But at least you can be sure of one thing, Alan McCarthy's not in any position to do you or your family any harm."

Brenda glanced at the policeman, still with a concerned look on her face.

"Are you absolutely sure about that?' she said brusquely, "Because I'm not!"

The ghostly telephone calls did continue right up until Brenda Gibson moved to another house. The people who bought the house from her also received the same ghostly calls for a period of about six months. Then, without any warning, they stopped completely. Maybe Alan McCarthy could not pay his phone bill and was cut off!

29

A DOUBLE TAKE

B i-location is the unusual and yet not so rare phenomenon of a person being seen in two places at the same time, whilst still very much alive.

Someone who was known to frequently bi-locate whilst he was alive was Padre Pio, the first stigmatised priest in the history of the Catholic Church. Padre Pio was born on the 25 May 1887, in Pietrelcina, in southern Italy. On the 20 September 1918 the five wounds of the crucifixion appeared on his body, a clear sign that this diminutive priest was quite special.

Padre Pio's life was marked by long hours of prayer and austerity and, although he did not enjoy very good health, his deep faith and belief in God sustained him. Towards the end of his life Padre Pio became quite frail, and he died on 23 September 1968, in San Giovanni Rotondo in Italy. Whilst Padre Pio was still alive he allegedly appeared to those who prayed to him for help, and frequently thousands of miles from where he himself lived. Although Padre Pio was an extremely special man with extraordinary powers, Henry Sattlethwaite was just an ordinary man and lived a very different life to Padre Pio, and yet many claimed to have seen him in two places.

Henry Sattlethwaite was a welder by profession, and lived with his wife Joan and two teenage daughters, Christine and Joanne, in Crosby. Although Henry was a decent man he had no particular beliefs and wasn't religious at all.

Henry's life began to change dramatically when he sustained a head injury at work and as a consequence was hospitalised for two weeks for routine tests, his wife had been told.

Henry Sattlethwaite was well-liked by his many work colleagues. During his two week stay in hospital he was exhausted with the many daily visitors and so was relieved when he was finally discharged. "You must take it easy," the consultant said. "You can expect to experience headaches for a while." Needless to say the consultant's advice went in one ear and out of the other, and within two days Henry was back at work.

Thinking that Henry was still off work recovering from his accident, neighbour Tom Lewis called to Henry as he was putting the key in his front door, and was quite surprised when he appeared to ignore him.

Pat Dodd, another neighbour, also remarked that Henry Sattlethwaite had ignored her when she let on to him whilst shopping. It was only when Henry's wife told them that her husband had gone back to work almost immediately that the saga became more embroiled in mystery and his wife began to worry.

Although the couple had been married for over twenty years, she suddenly became suspicious and wondered if the accident had caused him to behave out of character. It even crossed Joan's mind that her husband might be having an affair, but this notion was dismissed when she thought of how close they were.

Joan eventually told her husband about the concerns of their neighbours and friends, and it was clear from his face that he just did not know what to say. After giving it some thought Henry laughed. "They've been mistaken," he said. "I've never heard anything like it in all my life." Although Henry Sattlethwaite dismissed the whole thing as nonsense, Joan knew her husband well enough to sense that he was a little concerned.

The weeks passed by and two more episodes of the spooky phenomenon were reported to Joan, who was by now beginning to believe that there was more to it than she had previously thought.

"There must be something in it?' said Joan to her husband with concern, "too many of our friends have witnessed it."

'You're really spooking me now,' huffed Henry, shaking the creases from his Echo. 'I don't really know what to say.'

Joan decided to lay the matter to rest and never mentioned it to Henry again, even when her cousin, Lily, reported that he also ignored her whilst she was shopping in South Road.

As the sightings of Henry increased, he began to complain of severe headaches as the consultant had warned and Henry was beginning to feel depressed.

Henry Sattlethwaite had never driven in his life and had always travelled to his place of work in the city centre by bus.

It was just before 6pm and he was three hundred yards from home. As he turned the corner into his own street, he noticed two neighbours chatting on the doorstep, and another man walking towards him. Henry was more interested in his neighbours and was only vaguely aware of the man walking in his direction. Just when he was about to let on to the two women engrossed in conversation, he heard one of them shouting: "Hello, Henry. Feeling any better?" He stopped in his tracks when he realised the woman was talking to the other man and not to him.

Henry's eyes moved from the woman to the man now standing in front him. He froze to the spot as the man moved nearer and he then realised that he'd come face to face with himself.

The man stood in front of Henry and he looked dumfounded. Henry swung his head round to make sure that the two women had witnessed the eerie phenomenon, and he could see that they were both staring in disbelief. At that point Henry remembers nothing else. He woke up in a hospital bed where he remained for three days and was discharged after undergoing tests. He left the hospital with a clean bill of health: The headaches had gone, and so too had his doppelganger... forever.

> Billy says: During my research into the phenomenon of bi-location, I collected no fewer than forty stories of people who had experienced it, and all these were in the Merseyside area.

30

A Surprise From The Past

George Brindle had an almost fanatical passion for metal detecting. He was fascinated with the past and, to his wife's dismay, would spend most of his spare time with his friend, Jack Foster, detecting either on a farm somewhere on the outskirts of Liverpool, or occasionally on a Victorian rubbish tip in Heswall on the Wirral.

Apart from numerous old coins, several Saxon swords and an Elizabethan crucifix, George had unearthed nothing of any great value, but he was certain that one day his luck would change and he would discover an ancient hoard of diamonds and gold. This was his dream, but in reality he knew that that was all it was – a mere dream. Nonetheless, George Brindle loved his hobby and for those few hours on a Saturday and Sunday, he was always just a few feet away from an incredible discovery.

One Sunday morning on 3rd September 1988, as the weather did not look too promising, George and Jack decided that a local dig would be preferable. They settled for the Victorian rubbish tip by Old Nick's Cave in Sefton Park. This meant that afterwards they could call into the 'Albert' in Lark Lane for a pint or two before heading back home with their finds.

It was just after 9 o'clock in the morning and, apart from the odd jogger and man walking his dog, the park was fairly quiet.

George had found quite a number of small things of interest at this location, and both he and Jack were always excited over any find, regardless of whether it was a bent Victorian spoon, or the remains of an old pewter mug. Anything was a great discovery to the two enthusiasts, whose motto was 'It's not the finding so much as the looking'.

Only half an hour had gone by when George got a fairly strong response from his detector. After establishing the exact spot that was producing the signal, he began digging with his trowel. He had dug down a good twelve inches when he made contact with a tin object. Calling out excitedly to Jack and, without pausing for breath, he continued to prise his find free from the ground. It was some sort of a tin casket with a name engraved across the lid, 'Charles Langton Yates'.

"That's odd!" muttered George. "That was the name of a Victorian magician and mystic who lived in my house at the beginning of the century. He was apparently quite brilliant but also very strange."

"Open it," said Jack eagerly. "This might just be the find we've been waiting for."

"No such luck!" replied George. "It's probably empty."

Jack watched patiently as George forced the lid of the box open with the edge of his trowel and then reached inside to retrieve its contents.

"What is it?" asked Jack, as he impatiently watched George's muddy fingers clumsily opening a piece of faded parchment. The writing on it was now quite faint and George struggled to read it out loud to his friend, scarcely able to believe his eyes: "To George Brindle, who may stumble across this box. If he does, I will have achieved the impossible! I return the enclosed to your safe keeping and sincerely hope you will forgive me for any inconvenience I may have caused you. April 4th 1901. Charles Langton Yates, 27 Sydenham Avenue, Sefton Park."

"How is that possible?" gasped Jack with a puzzled frown.

George was speechless and his hand trembled as he retrieved a leather pouch from the box and emptied its contents into the palm of his hand. Feeling increasingly bewildered and confused, he examined the contents of the pouch: a gold signet ring and an eternity ring. His face turned pale as he recognised the rings.

"What is it, George?" prompted Jack, concerned. "Are you alright? You look as though you've seen a ghost."

"I have!" mumbled George as if in a trance. "These rings went missing from my house over ten years ago. They disappeared completely without trace. At the time I was out of work and Margaret accused me of selling them."

"But surely they can't be the same rings," said Jack incredulously. "This box has been buried for over eighty years."

'I'd know them anywhere.' He said nostalgically. 'The signet ring was my father's and I had it engraved with my initials. Look!" And he offered the rings to his friend for examination.

"Good grief! You're right!" Jack gasped, confirming the inscription. "GW – How is it possible?"

"The only person who can answer that is Charles Langton Yates," George concluded. "And he's not here – or is he?"

31

GHOSTS OF LIVERPOOL THEATRES

Although I have been appearing at the Neptune Theatre in Hanover Street with my Psychic Stage Shows since the late eighties, I first appeared there in 1963 with my band, the City Beats in the Frankie Vaughan Talent Competition, run by the Liverpool Echo.

It was then called Crane Hall and was above Crane's Music Shop, one of Liverpool's three thriving dealers in musical instruments, particularly pianos. As a matter of interest, Denny Seyton and the Sabres, the Senators and my band the City Beats, all got through to the finals held on the South Pier in Blackpool. Denny Seyton and Sabres won, the Senators came second and my band came third.

Although I was only seventeen, and my psychic abilities were then channelled into the creative areas of my life, they were still very active and frequently manifested themselves spontaneously.

My first ghostly encounter at the Neptune theatre was when it was Crane Hall and we had finished playing on the third night of the competition,

We had just walked off stage and were still very much under the influence of the adrenalin rush produced by all the excitement, when I bumped into a small gentleman in a dark suit. He had salt and pepper hair, heavily greased down with a central parting, and a thick moustache. I remember noticing the collar of his shirt, which was the old-fashioned, butterfly type, turned down at the corners with a black 'dickie bow' tie. He wore gold rimmed spectacles which were perched at the end of his nose and he peered over them at me with a warm smile.

"That was nice," he remarked, then continued to wend his way along the back of the stage.

"He was weird," I said to one of the guys standing by me. "Who is he I wonder?'

"Who's who?" came the reply.

"Him!" I pointed along the back of the stage but we could only see three other musicians waiting to make there entry onto the stage. The man had gone – disappeared completely. I thought no more of it and put the incident out of my mind.

Some years later in the 1980s I was giving my first Psychic Show at the Neptune Theatre, and was sitting alone in the dressing room with the door open. I saw the figure of a man pass by the door, making his way in the direction of the auditorium. Footsteps usually echoed at the back of the stage, but the man had not made a sound. This took place over an hour before the show was to begin and so the theatre itself was completely empty. I looked out of the dressing room door and could not see anyone. At that point I thought it might have been the stage manager, Dave Saville, getting the stage and lighting ready for the show, and expected him to call me any minute to do a sound check.

My curiosity led me along the short corridor and into the theatre, but again it was empty. Furthermore, I was informed by the assistant manager that Dave Saville had not yet arrived, and that she and only one other member of staff were there. No one had been at the back of the stage at all.

I was then standing in front of the stage waiting for the medium who was appearing with me to arrive, when I noticed a shadowy figure of a man on the balcony. This figure just seemed to disappear into nothingness and I could hear a man laughing, a sound which seemed to bounce of the walls of the empty theatre.

I later discovered that in the early part of the twentieth century, one of the theatre's assistant managers had collapsed and died on the balcony. I am quite certain that the man I had seen was him.

On another occasion at the Neptune, some years ago, I saw a lady and a young girl sitting in the theatre when it was empty. I went outside to enquire why they had been allowed in so early, and when I returned with the house manager they had gone. Some years ago a mother and her daughter were knocked down and both killed outside the Neptune, on their way to see a pantomime. Could it have been them?

I was told by some of the staff that they refuse to go into the green room to turn the lights out last thing at night, as some of them have seen the ghostly image of one of the Crane brothers staring out at them. He allegedly hanged himself in the Green Room and his ghostly apparition has appeared to many of the staff over the years. In fact, the Green Room is quite eerie even with the lights on, and it is obviously the epicentre for a lot of paranormal phenomena.

THE EMPIRE

Sitting backstage at the Liverpool Empire, it does not require much imagination to be transported back through time to when the city centre theatre was host to some of the greatest names of the stage.

They've all appeared at the Empire, from the legendry Mae West to Frank Sinatra. Although there have been reports of the ghost of Mae West appearing back stage, one wonders why on earth she would want to return to the Empire Theatre when she appeared in theatres all over the world.

However, there have been many ghostly sightings of Wee Georgie Wood, a diminutive comedy character who appeared on stage at the Empire many times. In fact, Wee Georgie Wood often announced that the Liverpool Empire was one of his favourite venues. Maybe this is why his ghost was seen there.

There have been numerous ghostly sightings at the Empire over the years, but one of the most consistent appearances over the past forty years is that of a little girl dressed in Victorian clothes.

She is frequently seen by staff wondering around crying in the stalls bar area when the building is closed. Occasionally she is seen being dragged by the apparition of a tall, well-dressed Victorian man with very dark eyes. Before the theatre was actually called The Empire a little girl allegedly fell to her death in the stalls. It is believed to be her ghost that is seen.

Other people claim to have seen the ghost of 1940s Liverpool comedy star 'Big Hearted' Arthur Askey, who frequently appeared at the Empire.

The appearance of a ghostly workman, who has been given the name 'Les', has also been reported at the Empire theatre He apparently was killed there many years ago and returns to 'haunt' the place where he worked.

THE MORE HUMOUROUS SIDE OF THINGS

I have appeared several times at the Empire with my psychic stage shows and was always uneasy sitting alone in the dressing room trying to relax before the show.

When I appeared there in 1998 I was asked by the News of the World if I would conduct a psychic experiment. Although I am often suspicious of any journalistic interest in my work, particularly when it involves one of the Sunday papers, I did accept the offer.

The News of the World had in fact heard that the Liverpool Empire was haunted by several ghosts and had invited a group of people from the Manchester Paranormal Society to investigate the phenomena. Although I explained to them that a séance was now somewhat old fashioned, and therefore belonged to the pages of an Agatha Christie novel, the newspaper insisted that I should conduct one for them.

After the show that night I was introduced to six young and very enthusiastic members of the Paranormal Society. I must admit, without being too rude, they were exactly what I expected, complete with a Miss Marple-type spokeswoman, who immediately threw herself into raptures over the 'marvellous atmosphere.'

"Can you feel the vibes?" she groaned, almost in ecstasy. "There's definitely a presence here."

Her companions stood around her in awe, rather like a guru surrounded by her devotees.

"Wow! Yes," they all sighed in agreement.

"It's quite strong over here," one of the young ladies suggested.

"And over here," said another.

I was totally exhausted from the evening's show and really just wanted to meet my friends in the theatre bar for a drink, before making my way home to where I then lived in Southport.

"Can you not feel it, Billy?" a very effeminate young man asked.

"Feel what exactly?" I answered with a tone of sarcasm.

"The presence," he replied.

"I can't say I can," I answered, feeling almost guilty.

We eventually got round to sitting in the dressing room where the séance was to be held.

"Shouldn't we be sitting in a circle?" asked one of the young men, "holding hands?"

Ever eager to please, I went along with the charade. At that point I realised that the journalist was getting a little impatient and so I went through the expected routine.

I honestly did not feel anything supernatural at all, but knew that the group of young paranormal enthusiasts were expecting something to happen. I began to hype it up a little, knowing quite well that the group gathered round me would go along with the whole thing.

Three of them began quaking, as though they had been overwhelmed by some unseen supernatural force, and it was all that I could do to stop myself from breaking into laughter. At that point the oval coffee table we were sitting around began to vibrate and, without actually lifting from the floor, it started to slide in my direction. My eyes moved around the circle just to make certain that no one was moving it, but no one was actually sitting close enough to the table.

I know I am not supposed to get spooked, but I was. And when the table moved close to me and then began to vibrate so fiercely against my legs that a vase that was neatly placed on the dressing table behind me crashed to the floor without breaking, I had had enough. I stood up and said: "I'm sorry folks, but I really must be going."

"Awesome," they all said in unison. "That was incredible."

I made my apologies to the journalist and then left for a few drinks in the bar.

I personally have seen quite a few so-called apparitions at the Empire Theatre over the years I have worked there. On one particular occasion I saw someone I would swear was Arthur Lucan, of Old Mother Riley fame. I encountered him at the back of the stage, dressed up in his Old Mother Riley clothes.

He brushed passed me and I could smell his stage make-up and another indescribable fragrance. As soon as I realised who it was passing by, I swung round to take a proper look but he'd just disappeared.

From a paranormal point of view, theatres are nearly always extremely active with discarnate energy. However, it is not always the actual spirit of the person who makes the ghostly appearance, for it is frequently no more than an emotional impression in the atmosphere that appears as a ghostly apparition.

THE THEATRE ROYAL

In my work as a stage psychic, I have appeared in hundreds of theatres and concert halls all over the United Kingdom, most of which were simply 'alive' with atmosphere and emotion.

In fact, most old theatres are permeated with the memories of the past and nearly always possess a charged atmosphere – an indescribable mix of emotion and passion that can often be frighteningly overpowering.

Although it is now very basic, a shadow of its former glory, one of the most psychically atmospheric theatres for me to work in is the Theatre Royal, in Corporation Street, St Helens. There is something about the Theatre Royal that always sends a rush of adrenaline through me, and never fails to leave me full of anticipation and excitement. Every time that I have appeared at the theatre I have experienced something different.

I always like to arrive at a theatre at least an hour-and-a-half before a show, as this way I know I will be totally relaxed, and ready for the psychic demonstration.

The first time that I did a show at the Theatre Royal I was sitting alone in the dressing room, preparing my mind for the show and I was completely lost in thought, just staring at the corner of the room.

I suddenly felt someone at the side of me, and when I turned my head, I noticed an elderly man standing there, staring at me with a wry smile on his face. He mumbled something almost incoherently, and when I sat forward to catch what he was saying, I noticed that his feet were not making contact with the floor, and that he seemed to be suspended about four inches in the air.

I sprang to my feet in alarm and the little man disappeared in front of me. I should have realised that the dressing door was on the right-hand side of the room, almost directly in front of me. No one could have entered the room without me seeing them and yet the little man was standing at the side of me, by the sink.

This was not something I experienced simply because I am a medium – if the phenomenon was the result of my clairvoyant ability the ghostly apparition would not have disappeared in this way, but would have remained until I had consciously closed it completely from my mind. I was certain that this was an objective ghostly manifestation and not a subjective one, and that the little man would have appeared to anyone who happened to have been there at the time.

On another occasion the ghostly apparition appeared to one of my guests on the show, who described him exactly as I had seen him previously. SPOOKYYYY!!

THE ROYAL COURT

Liverpool's Royal Court Theatre has had some of the most famous performers on its stage over the past fifty years or so.

Although today it is sadly a shadow of its former glory, it is allegedly still the home of a resident ghost in the form of an ex-caretaker who lost his life whilst clearing the debris from the roof on an icy day.

He is said to have slipped and broken his leg and as a consequence died of exposure. There have in fact been many sightings of this ghostly figure over the last twenty years, and he is now regarded as the theatre's resident ghost.

He obviously enjoyed his work so much that he continues doing it beyond the grave!

THE EVERYMAN THEATRE

The Everyman Theatre has a lot of historical form, and the present structure was originally built on a place of worship. In the 1960s it was known as 'Hope Hall' obviously an indication of its religious origins, and I played there with my band The Kruzads on numerous occasions.

Today though the Everyman bears little resemblance to its predecessor Hope Hall, even though the ghosts of bygone days are still in residence. Shadows and ghostly apparitions have frequently been witnessed over the years, and there have been reports of a malevolent male ghost who leaves behind the extremely unpleasant smell of urine. Even though the part of the building where the stench is said to linger has been fumigated, the cleansing process only lasts for a short while before the vile odour returns.

Although the ghostly apparition of the man has not been reported for some time, his footsteps are occasionally heard echoing through the empty building at night. Members of the staff at the Everyman have also reported seeing shadows in the men's toilet last thing at night when they are locking up the building, but when they investigate there is never anyone there. Some of the staff have claimed that when they are making their way to the exit doors at the rear of the building, hand driers go on by themselves in the toilets, and lights are seen going on and off.

What makes it even spookier is that the power source is always turned off from the lighting and sound room before the theatre is secured for the night.

THE LIVERPOOL PLAYHOUSE

This famous theatre has seen the appearances of many stars of stage and screen, from Laurence Olivier to Peter O'Toole. Like other theatres the Playhouse also has spectres that refuse to leave.

Before the Playhouse was granted its license in 1897, it was a music hall and variety theatre. It was then that a cleaner named Elizabeth was going about her chores on the stage when the fire iron fell and struck her on the head. She was killed immediately and has haunted the theatre ever since. Her ghostly form is frequently seen in the gallery level, particularly at seat A5, where witnesses report a coldness and eerie feeling.

A Grey Lady is also said to have been seen wandering from the stalls coffee bar area into the stalls seating area. She is said to be very refined and wearing a grey coat with a hood.

There have also been reports of the ghostly figure of gentleman dressed in a frock coat and wearing a top hat. His daughter apparently ran away to join the repertory theatre in the early 1900s against his wishes. He still seems to be searching for her.

Builders working on the refurbishment of the Playhouse in 1999 are said to have downed tools because of ghostly apparitions and noises. Electricians rewiring the theatre reported spooky goings on, such as water taps turning on by themselves and heavy doors opening and closing when there was nobody there. Ghostly shadows were also seen by the workmen in the basement.

Billy says: As a medium and paranormal investigator, I am quite certain that the majority of so-called hauntings are greatly exaggerated. Nonetheless, ghosts do exist and you can never know when or where you are being watched.

32

THE GHOSTS OF SPEKE HALL

Speke hall is a timber-framed house that was largely completed in 1598, and is situated in Speke Hall Road, approximately eight miles south of Liverpool, quite close to John Lennon Airport.

The first owner was Edward Norris of the famous Norris family, and the hall is allegedly haunted by the ghost of Mary Norris who committed suicide after throwing her baby into the moat whilst the balance of her mind was disturbed. In fact, Mary Norris married Sydney Beauclerk, a compulsive gambler who is believed to have made her life a misery and caused her to have a mental breakdown.

Although historical records confirm that whilst the Beauclerk family did purchase the house from the Norris family, the Beauclerks themselves never actually lived in Speke Hall. Nonetheless, Speke Hall has more than one ghostly inhabitant, Mary being one, her baby being the other.

My philosophy has always been 'seeing is believing,' which is why I accepted the invitation to conduct a ghost hunt in Speke Hall for charity some years ago. Although I was not allowed to remain in the house overnight, the time I did spend there late at night was sufficient for me to 'encounter' some of the ghostly residents. Although Speke Hall has been extensively restored by The National Trust, the character and paranormal atmosphere has not changed at all.

Armed with an EMF Meter (Electro-Magnetic-Frequency), a non-contact thermometer with laser and an extremely sensitive and very expensive camera, we set about catching ourselves some ghosts.

The night began with a guided tour conducted by one of the National Trust guides, who basically filled us in with all the historical facts, and then I was left to my own devices.

We wandered through the creaky corridors with the EMF to no avail at first, but then on the approach to the tapestry room it began to oscillate and the needle on the meter went berserk. This corresponded with a strange feeling of disorientation and then I glimpsed a lady in a long grey/blue dress who disappeared through the door leading into the tapestry room.

I also became aware of a man who looked very much like a gardener or a worker of some kind standing at the end of the corridor just by the staircase. He looked in his mid to late fifties, bald, wearing some sort of cloth jerkin secured around the middle with a leather belt. He was also wearing knee length boots. The funny thing was, unlike the majority of so-called 'ghosts', I am certain that he was aware of us as his eyes followed us and he even smiled.

At the end of the very late night I concluded that Speke Hall is certainly haunted and that no way would I sleep in that building by myself.

33

THE GHOST OF
THE FAIRY BRIDGE

E ver since I can remember, the iron bridge in Sefton Park was known to the locals as the 'Fairy Bridge,' because fairies allegedly lived there. Although the latter may not be quite true, of one thing you can be sure, it is truly an enchanted place.

A prize of 300 guineas was won by M Andre, a French gardener, and architect Mr Lewis Hornblower for designing and laying out some land in Liverpool for 'the delight and pleasure of the public'.

The competition was in 1866, and Sefton Park was officially opened by Prince Arthur, the third son of Queen Victoria, on May 20th 1872. Sefton Park was named after the Earl of Sefton, and is Liverpool's largest park, thought to be larger than any of the parks in London.

Apart from all this though, Sefton Park is said to be one of the most haunted parks in the United Kingdom.

Over the past seventy or so years, a young teenage girl in a white dress has been seen sitting under the cast iron bridge beside the stream, singing quite merrily to herself. One very warm summer's afternoon in the mid-sixties, a young couple were sitting by the stream enjoying the sunshine, when they noticed the teenage girl sitting not far from them. They hadn't noticed her before, nor had they seen her coming, but she ignored them and carried on singing. It was only when the couple had got up to leave that they noticed she had gone – disappeared.

There have been many sightings of the ghostly young girl

beneath the Fairy Bridge. Witnesses have described her as looking like Alice from Alice in Wonderland, fair haired with two plaits tied with a ribbon on each.

THE GHOST OF OLD NICK'S CAVE

In the late 1800s a young girl was murdered in Sefton Park in what has become known over the years as 'Old Nick's Cave'.

She was allegedly raped and strangled and the perpetrator of the gruesome crime was never brought to justice. The body of the twelve-year-old girl was found carefully hidden in the cave, then a beauty spot, and was discovered by children playing on a warm summer's day.

The murder quickly became a legend and was so well known in the Victorian times that a folk song was even written about it. The ghost of the little girl has been sighted on numerous occasions, usually late in the afternoon, when the murder is supposed to have taken place, and always in the summer.

Jack Smith was walking his little terrier by the caves one August afternoon in 1985. His little dog had wandered off in the direction of Old Nick's Cave, when he saw a young girl stooping to stroke it. When she saw Jack Smith approaching her, she suddenly looked quite frightened and ran into the cave (the caves were then open unlike today).

A little puzzled by the child's reaction, Jack clicked the lead onto his dog's collar to prevent it from wandering off again and moved closer to the cave's entrance to check the little girl was alright. He was quite surprised to see that the cave was completely empty and that she was nowhere to be seen.

Mavis Thomson was also taking a leisurely walk through Sefton Park with her husband, and they had just crossed the road in front of Old Nick's Cave when they noticed a dark-haired little girl playing there. As they made their way nearer to the caves, she disappeared through the entrance of the cave nearest to the road, just as on the previous sighting. Concerned that such a young child was on her own so late in the park, Jim Thomson paused to check that she was not lost, or in trouble, but again the cave was completely empty and the child was nowhere to be seen.

Over the years there have been many reports of the little girl's ghostly appearance. Even today, though the entrance to both caves has been securely sealed, she is still occasionally spotted entering the cave nearest the road.

If anyone can offer me any information about the murder of the little girl in Old Nick's Cave, please contact me via my website at www.billyroberts.co.uk

THE UNLUCKY TREE IN SEFTON PARK

It is really only over the past thirty years or so that it has become fashionable to mark the spot where someone has been killed with flowers. This ritual is generally accepted as a mark of respect, and in the majority of cases that's all it is.

However, occasionally the ritual becomes something completely different, and placing flowers in the same place on a regular basis can empower the spot, thus transforming the emotion into a negative magnetic force. One example is a certain tree in Sefton Park. The first accident occurred when a small car skidded on the icy December road and crashed into the tree. The middle aged driver was killed instantly. That was in 1975, and the first flowers were then laid.

No more than twelve months later the driver of a car travelling around the park late at night, misjudged the poorly lit road and crashed into the same tree. Although the driver survived the accident, he died of his injuries some days later. More flowers were laid, and continued to be laid. The third accident also took place in the seventies. This was a student jogging around the park, when a car careered off the road, knocking her down, and killing her instantly. More flowers were seen to be laid at the spot. And so the story goes on.

There were two fatalities very close to the tree in the eighties, and another jogger was killed there in the 90s. The tree seems to have been like a volcano waiting to erupt, and now things have been set in motion, I am sure there is more to come.

Also around the same area ghostly apparitions have been reported by late night joggers. One jogger going through his pace was stopped in his track by a young girl who just disappeared before him.

Removing the tree would not solve the problem, as the spot has already been empowered.

34

STOP THE CLOCKS

Jim Becket was a retired builder and spent most of his spare time either fixing or making clocks. In fact, he'd always had a fascination with clocks, ever since he was a child.

His parents had expected him to pursue his interest as a career. Unfortunately, one thing led to another and Jim found himself following his father's footsteps into the building trade instead. However, this did not stop him still collecting old clocks, and walking into his workshop in the small room at the back of his little house in Bagot Street was just like walking into a clockmakers shop.

The walls of the room were strategically lined with many different kinds of clocks, modern and antique. Row upon row of them, ticking and chiming and driving Jim's wife, Molly, almost out of her mind. There was nothing that Jim Becket did not know about clocks, and with a steady hand and a keen eye, he could fix almost any make, regardless of size or intricacy of mechanism.

It was Thursday afternoon and Molly had been to the shops on nearby Lawrence Road. Overladen with bags of shopping, she struggled to put the key in the lock, cursing her husband in a low voice for not hearing her coming and opening the door for her. Eventually she managed to push the door back and placed her shopping bags on the floor in the hall whilst she extricated the key from the lock.

A deadly hush suddenly overcame her and she paused for a moment to listen. She checked her watch and it was exactly 4 o'clock and yet she could not hear any of the usual chimes from her husband's huge and noisy clock collection.

She knew instinctively that something was not quite right and, leaving her shopping where it was, she dashed quickly into the back room, anxiously calling her husband's name. Before Molly had even got as far as the back room door, she saw Jim lying in a heap on the floor. She bent over to help him, but soon realised that he was dead.

A post-mortem was later carried out and it revealed that Jim Becket had died from a massive heart attack. All Jim's clocks had stopped exactly on the hour of 3 o'clock – was this the exact time that he had died?

Although Jim Becket's clocks never worked properly again after his death, his favourite, wall-mounted clock still chimes, for some strange reason, regularly every 29th October – Jim's birthday.

35

THE GHOSTLY BABY MINDER

In the 1950s Winnie Newkirk moved into a house in Coltart Road off Lodge Lane in Toxteth, Liverpool – a grand, three-story Victorian house, situated between Princess Park and Sefton Park.

Although she looked upon this as a new beginning, one of her main reasons for moving there was to be near her mother who lived in the house opposite and her sister Mary who lived just a few doors down the road.

The nanny to Winnie's three children also lived at the bottom of the road so as far as she was concerned, the location was ideal, especially as her husband, Rocky, was in the American Merchant Navy. He was frequently away for long periods as a consequence of the various wars in which America was involved at the time. Winnie missed her husband so much, but at least she had her mother and sister to keep her company.

Sometime around 1958, what seemed like an almost idyllic life changed for Winnie Newkirk when she fell quite poorly. The doctor's diagnosis was that her health problems were due to the fact that the mother-of-three had had two of her children in quick succession. However, to exacerbate things Winnie's sister, Mary, was diagnosed with leukaemia.

Within months Mary had passed away and Winnie was devastated. Not long after Mary's death Winnie was diagnosed with tuberculosis and had to be admitted to a sanatorium for treatment. With two very young children to look after she just did not know what to do. There seemed to be no alternative but to allow her two sisters to take them. As they lived in different countries, Winnie was reluctant to agree to this and so it was decided to put her two young children in a private nursery in Fulwood Park, Aigburth.

The problem seemed to be resolved, and Winnie Newkirk's run of bad luck seemed to be coming to an end. She was discharged from the sanatorium with a clean bill of health and although advised not to have any more children, Winnie did become pregnant, and on Monday 5th October 1964 she gave birth to a little girl, Donna Maria.

Life for the Newkirk family could not be better, and Winnie was now looking forward to a much brighter future.

One night Winnie was waiting for her husband, Rocky, to return home and her two children, Sheree and Denise had been playing somewhere in the house, when Winnie saw a shadowy figure lean over the banisters on the broad staircase. Thinking that it was her children misbehaving she shouted up the stairs to them. "I will tell your father! Get to bed NOW!"

With no response from her children Winnie went upstairs to see what they were up to, and was absolutely shocked to see them both tucked up in bed fast asleep. Although Winnie Newkirk was a staunch Catholic, she was very down to earth and not one who was frightened easily, and the eerie event was dismissed without further thought.

There were other spooky goings on at 81 Coltart Road, but Winnie was too busy looking after her young family and so just ignored the ghostly phenomena.

As baby Donna began to grow, Winnie couldn't help but notice that her young daughter would often talk to an imaginary person, and although Winnie herself could not see anybody, the conversations always seemed to be two-way.

Although she tried to dismiss this as childish imagination, she couldn't ignore other strange phenomena that were taking place around her young daughter. The playpen would unlock by itself, and the whole thing would rock backwards and forwards, almost playfully, as though moved by an invisible hand.

Winnie would never have believed it had she not witnessed it with her own eyes. She couldn't ignore the ghostly goings on around her daughter any longer, and although she was certain that whatever it was would not inflict any harm on her child, she still kept a vigilant eye on her.

Wherever young Donna was in the house, the ghostly figure of a man dressed in Victorian clothes could frequently be seen also. In fact, the young child would often be heard giggling and talking to her invisible visitor. When asked who she was talking to, Donna would simply answer: "The man over there."

As Winnie's child got older she was able to describe the man in more detail and explain to her mother exactly who he was. "He's my friend," she would announce. "He looks after me and tells me stories."

Donna's ghostly friend eventually became accepted as 'one of the family', and Winnie's child would often become very distressed if she was away from him for more than a day. The ghostly Victorian gentleman was extremely protective towards the young Donna and as she grew older their relationship became stronger.

The man's ghostly appearances were witnessed by most people in the family, and he really did become known as 'Donna's ghostly child minder'.

It was now clear to everyone that the ghost of 81 Coltart Road was much more than a child's imaginary playmate, and that he was Donna's invisible friend, a friend from another world – another time.

Winnie and Rocky Newkirk eventually decided it was time to move on, and so after giving it some consideration they bought a house in Mossley Hill. When they broke the news to their young daughter she became so distressed that they even considered abandoning their plans to move. However, a fresh start was needed and everything had been arranged.

Once all the furniture had been loaded into the removal van, Donna looked through the car window as it pulled away from 81 Coltart Road for the last time. She saw her Victorian friend staring sadly at her from the upstairs window. Donna knew then that she would never see her friend again.

Some time when Donna Newkirk was 16 and sitting for exams, she had a vivid dream that she had returned to her old home in Coltart Road to see her friend. In the dream he looked sad as he gestured around the room. Everything was black and burned, and Donna awoke from the dream feeling sad and depressed.

One day, her mother remarked to her sister-in-law that she would like to return 81 Coltart Road to see what it was now like. She replied: "That would be impossible, Winnie, it was burned to the ground and has now been completely demolished."

Donna still remembers her Victorian ghostly baby minder with great affection and knows that he is still there, somewhere, looking after her.

Billy says: This phenomenon is very common, and is an example of how Spirit People find it easy to interact with some children. However, the child must be psychically compatible with the so-called ghost to enable the phenomenon to take place.

36

THE GHOSTS OF A SHIP YARD

Cammell Laird's ship yard has seen the launch of many seagoing vessels during its life as a ship builder and one would expect it to have more than its fair share of ghosts.

Over the last 50 years or more workers at the famous ship yard have reported seeing the ghostly figure of an old woman wandering around the yard as though looking for someone, and when approached witnesses have claimed that she simply disappears without trace. Some believe that the old woman's husband was killed there in an accident a hundred years ago, and that her ghostly form wanders round still looking for him. She is frequently seen crying and looking very distressed.

Other phenomena occurring at the ship yard include lights turning on and off by themselves, ghostly shadows seen when there is no one there and disembodied voices echoing throughout the yard. Night workers have also reported ghostly figures in boiler suits disappearing into the night, and the apparition of a young man in his late twenties who was killed at the ship yard many years ago.

In the 1950s workers complained that tools were going missing and would turn up again in the most unlikely places and doors opened and closed by themselves. In fact, the ghostly phenomena are not just confined within the walls of Cammell Laird's ship yard. Many drivers have reported stopping to pick up a female hitchhiker in her mid twenties, almost outside of Cammell Lairds, and when asked how far she is going she always replies "Liverpool", even though she is travelling in completely the wrong direction. The young passenger simply disappears whilst driving along, leaving behind a sweet fragrance. The ghostly hitchhiker is believed to be a young girl who was knocked down and killed by a bus on the stretch of road outside of Cammell Laird's more than forty years ago. Although there have been no recent reports of her ghostly appearance, a description was given of a similar apparition on Telegraph Road, just outside of Heswall. In fact, the ghostly hitchhiker's description corresponds perfectly with that of the young girl picked up outside of Cammell Laird's, leading us to believe that they are one and the same person.

THE GHOST OF FORD'S

An ex-worker at the Halewood Ford factory told me of the ghost of the night shift that terrified all he nightworkers.

Some years ago now a man in his forties was working on nights in the 'press room', where the car body parts are actually pressed out, when a heavy crate suddenly fell from above and killed him outright.

Fellow workers have been spooked by the ghostly appearance of the man still busying himself in the press room, and some have even refused to remain in that part of the factory alone.

Other strange phenomena have also been reported by those working on nights, such as eerie shadowy figures appearing by machinery when the area is deserted, and a man's disembodied voice calling to his friend, who nobody seems to know.

37

THE LITTLE GIRL
WITH PIGTAILS

Even though the German bombers were systematically devastating the city of Liverpool in 1942, the spirit of the people and their instinct for survival remained strong and undaunted.

Visible signs of the war were apparent everywhere and there was not a street, or even a single house which did not bear the scars. In fact, in many areas, only desolation could be seen and the war-scarred streets of Wavertree, where Ken Luxton was born and had lived all his life, stood as a reminder that the whole country was under siege and was being savagely attacked by a ruthless nation which sought only to take control.

On one particular awful night, bombs had fallen more or less constantly and had devastated houses in Ash Grove, Ashfield and Wavertree Vale. Ken Luxton had been helping to search for survivors in the debris of a house in Ash Grove, where he also lived, and had stopped to drink a welcome cup of tea, which was being served by a group of locals at the roadside.

He stood pensively in complete silence, his eyes solemnly scanning the desolation before him, in horror and disbelief, only vaguely aware of the sounds around him, when he felt someone tugging insistently at his arm. He lowered his eyes to see a little girl with pigtails in her hair and the biggest pair of blue eyes that he had ever seen. She was very distressed and crying hysterically as she pulled at his arm, in an attempt to get him to follow her.

"Hang on there a minute, love, said Ken kindly, stooping to speak to her at her own height. "Now then, dry those eyes and tell me what's wrong?"

"My mummy's trapped in the cellar of our house," she sobbed. "Please help her. She can't move!"

"Right," said Ken urgently, "but first of all, tell me your name?"

"Linda," she sobbed, "Linda Goreman."

"Ok, Linda," he continued. "My name's Ken. Show me exactly where your mummy is and we'll have her out in no time."

Without another word being spoken, the little girl ran off through the debris at the corner of Ash Grove, pausing for a moment to make sure that Ken was close behind. He followed her into the entry at the back of the corner grocer's shop and along another entry leading into Wavertree Vale. She stopped abruptly by the remains of what had once been a house at the corner of the entry and urgently beckoned Ken to the spot. He could see immediately that the building had been reduced to rubble in the previous night's raid and he doubted if anyone could possibly have survived such an impact.

"She's in there," cried the little girl. "My mummy's trapped in the cellar with Laddie, my doggie. Please help her. Please get her out."

Ken paused for a moment whilst his eyes surveyed the devastation before him and, despite his pessimistic assessment of the situation, he tried to reassure her.

"Don't worry, love, your mummy will be alright," he said. "We'll get her out. You just stand over there so you won't get hurt should any of the rubble fall."

He picked his way cautiously towards the entrance to the cellar of he house, scrambling over the bricks and debris, pausing for a moment to check that the little girl was at a safe distance. He could see that she was waiting anxiously at the roadside and so continued to claw his way forward. There was no question that the house had taken a direct hit, which usually meant no survivors. Ken's task seemed almost futile but he knew that he just had to continue for Linda's sake.

It was obvious that he needed some help to clear the bricks and huge slabs of concrete that were blocking his way into the cellar of the house, but time was of the essence if there was to be any hope of a successful rescue.

Losing all track of time, he dug furiously and completely forgot about the little girl. As the minutes turned into hours, his clothes became stuck to his body with sweat and he ached so much that he felt as though he was about to collapse.

But, just when he thought that he could continue no longer, he detected a muffled voice coming from beneath the rubble. He held his breath and stopped digging for a moment to listen, but all he could hear was the occasional sound of falling bricks and cracking timber. He was just about to resume his efforts, when he heard the voice again.

"Please, please help me…"

He lowered his ear to the place where he thought the sound was coming from and then he yelled as loudly as he could.

"Keep shouting!" he urged. "Keep shouting so that I can work out exactly where to dig."

"Please help me," came the woman's voice again. "Help me."

The voice seemed to get louder each time it called out and, with each call, Ken Luxton gathered more and more strength. Within minutes, he had somehow cleared a way into the cellar and had pulled the woman and the dog clear of the rubble and out into the daylight. Although very badly shaken and more than a little bruised, Linda's mother was basically unharmed and was hugely relieved to see Ken's smiling face and to be out in the fresh air once again.

"Thank God!" she gasped, as he helped her to pick her way unsteadily over the rubble to the pavement. "Thank God you saved me. How on earth did you know I was down there?"

Ken laughed, overcome with emotion and understandable pride at his life-saving achievement.

"Nobody would ever have known you were there, had it not been for your little girl!" and he smiled broadly and turned to look for Linda.

"Little girl?" said the woman, puzzled. "What little girl?"

"Your little girl," retorted Ken, suddenly wondering if she had been concussed in the bombing.

"What did she look like?" asked the woman, obviously confused.

"Oh, about so high," said Ken indicating the little girl's height with his hand. "She had two pigtails and the biggest blue eyes I have ever seen. She said her name was Linda."

A tear suddenly trickled down the woman's cheek, cutting a little river through the dust and grime which covered her from top to toe and the little girl's name fell almost silently from her lips.

"Linda!" she whispered, a slight trembling smile parting her lips. "My little Linda. She was killed in the first twelve months of the war."

"But I saw her with my own eyes," insisted Ken. "I actually spoke to her and touched her."

"My Linda!" repeated the woman. "My precious little girl…"

38

The Ghost of a Jilted Bride

As a child I used to listen intently as my mother told me stories that would invariably send shivers down my spine, even though some of her tales seemed far too incredible to be true.

This story, however, coincided with one my aunt Louise told me only a few years before she died, and is the tale of a jilted bride who allegedly turned her back on life.

Somewhere around the early part of the twentieth century Margaret Rose Davis lived alone in a large three-storey house on the corner of Mulgrave Street and Upper Parliament Street. Miss Davies was to be married to a Liverpool solicitor by the name of Peter Swainson, but he allegedly left her waiting at the church, obviously having had second thoughts about the wedding.

Margaret Rose Davis was understandably devastated and upon returning to her home alone, is said to have closed her front door on the outside world forever.

The very beautiful Miss Davis is believed to have left the wedding table exactly as it was, laid with food, drink and a wedding cake and even wore her wedding dress until the day she died, a wizened and very bitter old lady.

My aunty Louise always said she remembered the house in the 1930s, with grimy windows and moth-eaten curtains, and an old front door that had been closed for many, many years.

Although the location of my mother's story was in a completely different part of Upper Parliament Street, it was essentially the same, but the ghost of this jilted bride allegedly persecuted the man who broke her heart, until he hanged himself in the basement of his home in Bentley Road.

39

Haunted Pubs in Liverpool

The Slaughterhouse

In 2004 Daily Post journalist, Mike Chapple, invited me to accompany him to the Slaughterhouse pub in Fenwick Street, where paranormal activity had been reported in the basement.

Although the Slaughterhouse has been a hostelry since 1723, before that it was allegedly a cattle slaughterhouse, as its name today suggests, and so as well as anything else, it did have a lot of historical atmosphere.

Mike explained that the manager of the pub had expressed an interest in me visiting his establishment in the hope that I would 'clear' whatever paranormal activity was there. It was suggested that I should bring along my usual ghost-busting gadgets, primarily as visual aids to reassure the staff and manager. As the manager of the Slaughterhouse was a self-confessed sceptic, I did initially think that he had only invited me as a publicity stunt to increase the clientele of his pub, but as it happened this turned out to be far from the truth.

Bar staff had complained of seeing intense white lights or orbs as they have become fashionably known, and the figure of a man dressed in 18th century-style clothes and a three-cornered hat, walking around in the basement as they were clearing the tables before closing last thing at night.

I must say, whenever I am invited to a so-called 'haunted' location I always like to wander quietly around by myself at first, as in this way I am left to drawer my own conclusions. Usually in these situations people tend to try and influence a medium's judgement by telling them what they have seen, instead of allowing the medium to tell them what is really there. This is how it works for me, and I do try to be as honest and blunt as people will allow.

Whilst I felt very little in the bar upstairs, downstairs in the entertainment area was a completely different story. As I walked onto the small stage I was immediately overwhelmed with a feeling of disorientation and foreboding. I then became aware of a very aggressive elderly gentleman, probably from the eighteenth century.

He had apparently been killed in the building in some sort of freak accident, and now found himself in a sort of a spiritual dilemma – lost between two worlds. I found it fascinating that there were other spirit entities, all from different periods of history and, although they were all aware of me, they were not aware of each other. There was also a lady who had apparently worked there as a barmaid in the early nineteenth century, and she appeared extremely distressed because she was unable to find her little girl. One of the ghostly figures was that of the pub's previous managers who had hanged himself sometime during the mid-19th century, and was still unable to come to terms with what he had done.

As well as the EMF meter going crazy, we also caught some very interesting light anomalies on the camera, showing significant fluctuations in the electro magnetic atmosphere.

We left the pub around 3am and my friend and I both concluded that the Slaughterhouse was indeed haunted. Although it was the manager's initial intention for me to 'clear' the atmosphere I was quite certain that this could not be done. Anyway, the ghostly inhabitants were not doing any harm whatsoever and, as far as I was concerned, they had as much right to be there as everyone else.

THE DEAD HOUSE

The Earle Hotel at the corner of Webster Road and Earle Road, to my mind, has always been affectionately known as 'The Dead House'.

One reason for the strange epithet was that funeral parties used to call there for the customary drink on their way to and from the cemetery in Smithdown Road. Another, more interesting and most certainly far more sinister, reason for the name is believed to be because of the unexpected demise of more than one of its licensees over the years.

In the mid-to-late 1940s at least two of the managers allegedly hanged themselves either in the cellar or in the flat upstairs. Although they were not in anyway connected to each other, these extremely sad and unfortunate occurrences somehow preceded a long line of unlucky events for the subsequent licensees.

All those either living or working in the pub were apparently plagued with bad luck that only ended when they actually left the pub. More than one licensee allegedly committed suicide in the Earle Hotel and in the mid-1950s there were reports of supernatural happenings in the cellar. Lights allegedly switched on and off by themselves (a common phenomenon where there is paranormal activity) and footsteps were heard in the empty pub at night.

In 1950 one barmaid claimed to have had an encounter with a man dressed in what she described as a foreign soldier's uniform. During the Second World War the Earle Hotel, like many other pubs in Liverpool, was the meeting place for American, Canadian and even Russian soldiers, who would congregate there on Saturday night.

From the barmaid's description of the ghostly soldier's uniform, it would seem that she had come face to face with a Russian airman. The same barmaid stayed after hours one night to clear up the glasses after a group of 21st birthday party revellers had finally left the pub. Walking into the snug, she noticed a little old man sitting on his own, drinking a glass of Guinness. After telling the man that last orders had long since been called, she turned her attention to the glass-laden table opposite him and set about clearing it.

When she glanced back again to chat to the old man, he had disappeared completely. Even his glass of beer and the empty bottle had gone. That was the final straw for her. Needless to say, she left the Earle Hotel immediately and never returned.

WOOLTON HALL

I was first invited to Woolton Hall in 1983 by the owner's wife, Jackie Hibbert, primarily for me to cast my psychic eye over the old place.

Although she and her family were quite happy living there, as they did at the time, she had told me of the ghost of monk, in Wellington boots, whom she and members of the staff had seen there over the years.

The monastic phantom was in no way malevolent and somehow seemed to possess a very wry sense of humour when he appeared unexpectedly, often in the dead of night.

The magnificent and most impressive Woolton Hall was partly designed by Robert Adam (of fireplace fame), and stands in its own grounds, set back and hidden from Speke Road by a tall sandstone wall. In fact, it was mostly because of the whole ambience and atmosphere surrounding Woolton Hall that I first decided to use it for seminars and psychic shows. I have been using it now for various events for over twenty years and, although I have never been fortunate enough to actually see the ghost of the monk, I have truly come to look upon Woolton Hall as home, and its owners as my friends.

Woolton Hall has been the location for various television programmes in which I have been involved over the years, and when I was asked to find a suitable location in which to film one of my paranormal videos, Woolton Hall immediately sprang to mind. I just knew the film company would be impressed with my choice of venue and I was right.

We spent three days filming and presenting various aspects of the paranormal, and even I was not prepared for what was about to happen. The producer asked me to walk about the hall from room to room and to relate my psychic impressions to the camera. To make it more interesting, they asked me to sensationalise the whole thing and to embroider what I was experiencing.

'This makes good viewing,' said the producer. 'You've got to do it, Billy.' But I could not, and furthermore I would not! However, I did feel quite confident that something would happen, and on the second day of filming I felt somewhat agitated all morning and I did not know why.

The cameras followed me up the broad staircase to the little room where I held my meetings every Thursday. This was my little sanctuary and I was sure that the room would feel somehow betrayed by the intrusion. We began filming, and with my back to the ornately designed fireplace, I began to deliver my piece into the camera. The crew consisted of two cameramen, two sound engineers and two producers, each of whom was busy tending to his own particular job.

Suddenly, and without prior warning, a glass of which had been placed on the mantelpiece by one of the producers, lifted into the air and was propelled across the room in front of the camera, smashing into pieces against the wall. One of the producers was so shocked that he was the first to run from the room, rapidly pursued by the rest of the crew.

They huddled on the landing outside, nervously puffing their cigarettes and debating whether or not to continue filming in the same room. I persuaded them to bring the first part of the video, at least, to its conclusion in the same room, and then we broke off for lunch.

Although they were making a series of videos about the paranormal, the main producer and the camera crew were extremely sceptical about the whole subject. I am convinced that the glass incident happened to force them to approach the making of the video with a more serious and less biased attitude. Luckily, most of it was caught on video, and when the footage was replayed, a bright flash of light could be seen following the glass as it moved quickly through the air. This was a prime example of telekinesis, and proved to the sceptical camera crew once and for all that this subject cannot in any way be taken lightly.

However, there was more to come. Apart from the manager of Woolton Hall, we were now in the building alone. Derek, one of the cameramen, took a break to visit the toilet and was surprised to find himself standing next to a man dressed in an evening suit. Thinking that perhaps the well-dressed gentleman was at some sort of function in another part of the hall, he paid no more attention to him.

Then the man asked Derek for the time, and when he turned his head to answer him, he had disappeared. Derek then realised that it was only 10am, and far too early for any functions to be taking place. He even checked in the corridor, but there was absolutely no sign of the well-dressed man anywhere. He resumed his position behind the camera, ashen-faced and trembling, before telling us the whole story. I could only laugh, as nothing really surprised me at Woolton Hall.

Later I asked John Hibbert, the manager of Woolton Hall, if there were any Masonic meetings on that night, to which he replied, 'No, I'm all alone tonight.'

Whenever I am asked 'Is Woolton Hall haunted?' I have to reply, 'Isn't everywhere?'.

Billy says: I have always had a special affection for Woolton Hall, and I suppose I got used to its atmosphere. However, I do know that it is haunted, most probably by the ghosts of those who enjoyed visiting the old manor when they were alive. In fact, the atmosphere was always different each time I visited Woolton Hall. Sometimes it was quite calm and peaceful, and other times I felt I was being watched each time I climbed the broad staircase on my way to gents.

40

When is a Haunted House Not a Haunted House?

When someone informs you that you are being taken to a haunted location, long before you arrive there your mind has already created its own ghosts and demons.

In fact, the mind is the common denominator where the paranormal is concerned, and once the suggestion has been implanted in the mind the imagination often takes over. It is possible to hype someone into such frenzy that he or she will swear that they have seen a 'ghost' even if the house is not actually haunted.

Now, let us make a detailed analysis of the so-called 'haunted phenomenon', and see what it is that really causes paranormal phenomena.

First of all, not all ghostly apparitions are earthbound spirits, revisiting the place where they once lived. They may be no more than a sort of photographic image in the subtle atmosphere, and appear to us just like watching a film on a DVD or video.

The electro-magnetic waves in the surrounding atmosphere capture sounds and images, in the same way that the magnetic coating on a video or audio tape can record them. The subtle structure of a building is very often impregnated with the images and sounds of the past, and these are more than likely stored in a sort of 'psychic memory bank', which can be accessed or triggered at any time.

This is not to say though that all apparitions are the products of electro-magnetic waves. On the contrary, some so-called ghosts are very real and do have the power to make their presence felt!

Occasionally ghostly manifestations can be the result of a geological phenomenon called 'triboluminescence', the friction of two quartz deposits below ground level.

This geological phenomenon affects the electro-magnetic atmosphere, sufficiently to create a disturbance in the brains of some people and so cause them to hallucinate.

The phenomenon of triboluminescence can also precipitate the electro-magnetic atmosphere sufficiently to 'open up' a portal to the spirit world, thus allowing ghostly phenomena to occur.

Research has shown that individuals who suffer from temporal lobe epilepsy are more susceptible to the effects of the phenomenon of triboluminescence, and may even have psychic experiences as a consequence of living in a geologically affected house.

INTERESTING FACTS

THE COMPLEXITIES OF THE HUMAN BRAIN

When you are frightened, as is the case in a so-called 'haunted' house, the electrical circuitry of the brain is affected and the surrounding electro-magnetic atmosphere is then disturbed as a direct consequence.

The mind may then be in such a state that you will be sure that you have either 'seen' or even 'heard' a ghost. The now very clichéd saying 'It's all in the mind', is more true than you might imagine, and a close analysis of your ghostly experience will probably reveal that what you actually think you saw was a subjective and not an objective phenomenon at all, proving after all that it really was 'all in the mind'!

SCIENTIFIC RESEARCH

Research done in Russia in the early part of the 20th century into the workings of psychic phenomena and the brain produced conclusive evidence that there was a significant abnormality in the electrical circuitry of the brain of someone who has psychic skills.

It was also discovered that the pineal gland – the walnut shaped gland deep within the brain – was probably responsible for psychic experiences. Professor Tutinsky's several years of research into paranormal experiences revealed that the pineal gland was much larger in the brain of a child than it was in an adult, and marginally more developed in a female than it was in the male.

This, the notable professor concluded, was most probably the very reason why children are traditionally more psychic than adults and why women are far more psychically sensitive than men. Tutinsky also concluded that, contrary to popular belief, being psychic is far from normal and that there is a noticeable abnormality in the brain of the person who is mediumistically inclined. In other words, seeing so-called 'dead' people is far from normal!

THE PHENOMENON OF THE AURA

One of the most misunderstood and frequently misused words in the psychic vocabulary is 'aura', and although the majority of people have a superficial understanding of its meaning, only a minority comprehend exactly what the phenomenon actually is.

We frequently say, 'The house has an aura of peace about it.' Or, 'He/she has an aura of calm.' And so we do use the word 'aura' to describe the general ambience of either a place or a person.

To begin with, the word 'aura' is far more than a descriptive term. It is a scientific fact – a metaphysical phenomenon – and is responsible for most if not all of human psychic experience. Scientifically, the aura is best described as a vaporous mass of electro-magnetic particles surrounding both animate and inanimate things. However, the aura surrounding the human form differs in more ways than one from that surrounding inanimate matter, in as much as the human aura represents the degree of life and consciousness present.

Although life is still present in inanimate matter, albeit at a lower level, the aura surrounding this is dull and lifeless, in comparison to the human aura which is full of colour and movement.

How Do We Know The Aura Exists?

Sometime in the twentieth century, Semyon and Valentina Kirlian, a husband and wife team from Krasnodar near the Black Sea, developed a camera which was capable of producing a monochrome photograph of the aura around the hands.

Although a crude apparatus, this camera enabled the Kirlians to make a detailed analysis of the aura and as a result they discovered that the small flairs of energy apparent around the hands, as seen in the photograph, somehow corresponded to the 700 points on the skin as charted in Chinese acupuncture.

This allowed the Kirlians to make an accurate diagnosis of disease. At the time, this was an inspiration to all those working in the same field. And so now you should have a fairly good idea of exactly what the aura is.

Everything and everybody has an aura, and it is through the aura that you are able to sense an impending doom or disaster, or know if somebody likes you or not. When two people are attracted to each other, their individual aurae are perfectly synchronised, giving a whole new meaning to the saying 'chemical attraction'.

Medieval artists knew about the aura and they depicted part of this in the 'halo' they painted around the heads of saints and other exalted beings. The multi-coloured feathered headdress of the Native American chief was also a symbolisation of the aura, and represented his spirituality and exalted position in the tribe.

In the early fifties Russian researchers referred to the aura as the 'human bioluminescence,' and regarded it as a sort of blueprint of the health. This was seen as a scientific breakthrough and an innovation at the time.

A detailed analysis of the bioluminescence enabled the researchers to access an incredible store of personal data relating to the individual. A full profile of the psychological and physical health, as well as a review of the emotional and spiritual natures, could be accessed through the aura's bioluminescence. The researchers also concluded that so-called 'ghosts' have a bioluminescence and that it is this phenomenon that makes them so apparent in the dark.

41

THE GHOST OF
SYDNEY HARGREAVES

Although I have never been interested in football, I was told this true story some years ago by my aunt Louise, a police woman and an avid Liverpool fan, as well as a Spiritualist.

Although Everton Football Club was founded in 1857, they actually held their matches at Anfield from 1884 in what is now Liverpool's ground. John Houlding was then the leaseholder of the Anfield ground but eventually purchased it outright.

As a consequence of rising costs to maintain the ground to its high standard, in 1884 the rent was increased from £100 and by 1890 it had reached £250. This left the Everton club no option but to make alternative arrangements, and so they left Anfield and moved to Goodison Park, where they are today. John Houlding was left in a difficult position. He had an empty football ground and only three players left in his team. With bills to pay, desperate measures were called for and so Houlding formed his own football team on 15 March 1892 and Liverpool Football Club was born.

All this is perhaps common knowledge to Liverpool and Everton supporters. As someone who has never followed football, I am perhaps in a minority, in Liverpool at least. However, I have always been amazed just how fanatically loyal Liverpool and Everton fans are to their respective teams and wonder what makes them like this when, after all, their grounds are both in Liverpool and only a stone's throw away from each other.

However, one man whose loyalties were perhaps not so cut and dried, and whose dilemma sent him completely over the edge, was 54-year-old groundsman, Sydney Hargreaves from Sleeper's Hill.

Along with James Roberts, he had been employed by John Houlding to keep the ground at Anfield tidy and in good order, but when Everton moved to Goodison Park and Liverpool Football Club was formed, everything suddenly changed for Sydney Hargreaves. Although a supporter of Everton Football Club, he had been at the Liverpool ground since the very beginning and did not really want to turn his back on John Houlding, even though the Everton Club offered him a job at their new ground. Sydney Hargreaves lived alone in a flat on Sleeper's Hill and had always been regarded as a bit strange by those who knew him.

He began drinking more than usual, and would often be seen in the Bronte public house, where he would stay until closing time. Although he had always been a conscientious worker and someone who had loved his job, he began staying off work so much that he was eventually fired.

This was the last straw for Sydney Hargreaves, who thought his life was over. Everton Football Club had been his whole life, but now that Liverpool had been established he found himself in an awful dilemma. He was confused and felt his loyalties were now divided between the two teams. Sydney had been out of work for more than two years and would often be seen making his way in a drunken, bewildered state between the two grounds. Ironically, Sydney Hargreaves was knocked down and killed by a dray horse and cart on the corner of Anfield Road and Sleeper's Hill, very close to his home.

No more than three weeks after his funeral, the ghostly figure of Sydney Hargreaves was seen at Liverpool football ground's main entrance and almost at the same time he was also seen at the entrance to the Everton ground. Sydney Hargreaves was even known to the local constabulary and Sergeant Dan Mclocklen could not believe his eyes when he came face to face with him whilst he walking his beat outside the Liverpool ground. Sergeant Mclocklen swore that Sydney Hargreaves looked him straight in the eyes as though he recognised him and 'did not seem like a ghost at all'. The burly Irish police sergeant was dumbfounded when the ghost of Sydney Hargreaves just disappeared before his eyes. He was so shaken that he had to call into the nearest hostelry to have something to steady his nerves (any excuse).

That was not the last time the ghost of Sydney Hargreaves was seen. In the 1920s and 30s there were several reports of sightings of a ghostly figure working on the grounds of both Everton and Liverpool and each eye-witness claimed that the apparition disappeared when it was disturbed.

The descriptions given of the ghostly figure left no doubt that it was the ghost of Sydney Hargreaves who had decided to divide his duties between Everton and Liverpool football clubs (problem solved for Sydney Hargreaves!).

42

EERIE ANIMAL TALES

The belief that we are a nation of animal lovers was truly proved to me when I began collecting unusual stories of animals.

I received hundreds of emails from people all over Merseyside wanting to tell me their remarkable stories about their pets from beyond the grave. Unfortunately, I have only been able to list some of them, but I am certain that the others will be included in a book specifically about animals. Anyway, remember, 'A house without a pet is just a house!'

THE CAT THAT PRAYS

Although I have always been a dog person, because of circumstances over the past seven years I have become quite accustomed to cats and have been fortunate to share my life with three very different feline personalities.

Pesi is a 16-year-old black and white pussycat with a very different, individual character. Pesi's mother was a cross between a streetwise tom and a refined Siamese cat.

To say that Pesi is extremely vocal is perhaps an understatement, as this very energetic and extremely youthful 16-year-old cat most certainly likes to be heard, and very often in the early hours of the morning too. In fact, Pesi can frequently be heard, in the middle of the night, loudly crying like a baby.

One particular night, just before midnight, I heard Pesi crying in her usual way and went upstairs to investigate. She sounded like a banshee, and I was certain she was distressed about something. Pesi was sitting on the dressing table in front of an old figure of St Teresa; her head was bowed, and it looked to all intense purposes as though Pesi was praying. I must say, it sent a shiver down my spine, especially that she seemed oblivious to my presence and continued crying for a further five minutes.

I would have thought that it was a one-off had she not repeated it several times after that. Even then we could have been forgiven for thinking that her actions were coincidental had she not started to move her attention to a crucifix on the landing wall. I am quite convinced that Pesi prays and often does so before she beds herself down for the night. Pesi is an extraordinary cat who obviously believes in whatever she prays to.

THE CHURCHGOING DOG

Barbara Jones had had Ben, her little brown and white mongrel dog, since he was six weeks old. He was now fifteen and showing signs of old age.

Barbara had noticed just how much Ben had slowed down over the last six months and was dreading the day when she would lose him. He was one of the family and her children loved him.

Ben was allowed to come and go as he pleased, and over the years had become quite a personality in the neighbourhood. In fact, everybody knew Ben, who could often be seen playing with the children, either on the corner of the street, or on the playground of St Martin's school.

Barbara always knew where Ben was and he very rarely strayed far. Ben was a creature of habit and always knew exactly when it was time to be fed. However, things suddenly changed one late afternoon when, to Barbara's surprise, Ben failed to come home as he always did at 5pm prompt. She searched the streets frantically, praying that nothing had happened to him. After she had exhausted all Ben's favourite places, she decided that it was best to return home. As she began making her way towards her front door, she heard someone call her from across the street. "Are you looking for Ben?" her neighbour asked. "Only I've just seen him in the church."

"In the church?" replied Barbara, somewhat puzzled. "Which church?"

"St Martin's," smiled the woman. "On Stapleton Avenue. Do you know where that is?"

"Yes, I know where it is," she said quickly. This was her church and also the church in which she had been married. "How strange!" Barbara thought, knowing full well that Ben did not know that – how could he?

As St Martin's was quite a distance from where she lived, Barbara decided to drive there. This would also make it easier to get Ben home. Sure enough, just as her neighbour had said, Ben was in the church, lying in the centre aisle in front of the altar rail. As soon as she called her dog he immediately ran to her wagging his tail.

Thinking that it was just a coincidence, Barbara thought no more about her dog's visit to the church until he went missing again three days later. Just as before she found Ben in St Martin's church, lying in exactly the same place in front of the altar rail. This time, however, she began to think there was more to it. In fact, this became a regular occurrence every two or three days. Barbara became so used to it that she just left him to return home by himself.

Four months went by and, sadly, Ben suddenly died of heart failure. Although they knew it had to come one day, Barbara and her family were heartbroken. She couldn't help think of Ben's visits to the church and wondered why he had chosen that particular one. Then, one day she had a visit from St Martin's priest, Father McGillin.

"I heard about your dog Ben," he said sympathetically.

Even though Barbara was no longer in St Martin's parish, she was christened there and it was also where she had married her husband Phil. But how did the priest know her dog's name? She looked at him curiously.

"Ben often visited my church," he continued. "He would just lie in front of the altar. I'm quite sure he was praying."

"Praying?" retorted Barbara with surprise at what she was hearing.

"Yes, praying!" He replied, a serious look on his face. "The cleaner first saw him and was all set to chase him into the street. But then she noticed the look in his eyes."

"Look?' she said. 'What do you mean?"

"I can't really explain. She called me to take a look at him and he just looked so peaceful. We decided he was doing no harm. But then he returned a few days later and sat in exactly the same place in front of the altar rail. He often came. I thought he was a stray and took a look at his collar. That's how I knew his name."

"Oh, I see," answered Barbara. "Thank you for letting me know."

"He was quite a special dog, I'm sure of that," remarked the priest.

'I know,' said Barbara sadly, a tear showing in the corner of her eye. 'He was very special.'

BESS RETURNS FROM BEYOND THE GRAVE

Bess was an old Labrador and Len Oates' constant companion since the death of his wife three years before.

Man and dog had developed a very special relationship in which Len swore each knew exactly what the other was thinking. Len would speak to Bess as though she were human and he knew that she understood his every word.

Bess was obedient, loving and loyal, and very rarely strayed far from her doting master's side. Len had come to rely on her more and more since his heart attack 18 months before. They went everywhere together, and on the odd occasion when Len left Bess at home, she would always be waiting for him by the window on his return. Bess loved her three outings a day on the common across the road – hail, rain or snow, Len never disappointed her.

Four days before Christmas Len was in bed suffering from the flu, so the job of walking Bess had been handed to Len's next door neighbour, a kindly lady who looked in on him several times a day.

On their return from the common Bess collapsed and died. Of course Len was absolutely devastated and did not know how he would be able to face life without his dearest friend.

Over the weeks that followed Len fell into a deep depression and, deprived now of his reason to go out every day, he refused to set foot over the doorstep. He cut himself off from everyone. He stopped eating and eventually could see no point in going on. Len became so ill that his only daughter came from the south of England to stay with him in Huyton.

One night whilst lying in bed unable to sleep, just staring sadly into the darkness of his room, Len suddenly heard a shuffling sound beside his bed. Before he could move a weight settled on his feet. Peering anxiously through the dim light to the end of the bed Len simply could not believe what he saw there: Old Bess was lying stretched across his feet, just as she had always done.

Convinced that he was dreaming, Len sat forwards to stroke Bess and was instantly shocked to feel her warm, familiar fur. Bess immediately stood up and scrambled along the bed towards him. With tears streaming down his face Len put his arms around her and hugged her. He knew this was no dream. Bess was 'alive' and warm and sitting in front of him. But, after only a moment, she jumped down from the bed and faded away into nothingness as Len watched.

When he awoke the next morning Len felt like a new man. His daughter was surprised when she came into the kitchen to find her father already washed and shaved and ready to take an early morning walk across the common, something he had not done since Bess's death. For Len now knew that Bess would always be there somewhere by his side and he had no intention of disappointing her.

"She's alive!" he told me. "She's alive somewhere and I know we'll all be together again someday."

Most people, no matter how much they have loved their pet, are not lucky enough to experience what Len experienced. Bess somehow managed to manifest to him, most probably because she knew just how ill he had become following her death. Her appearance certainly had a hugely positive effect on Len, both emotionally and physically.

> Billy says: The story of Len and Bess is one of many true stories I have collected over the years. The last time I heard Len was preparing to leave Liverpool to live with his daughter in Kent.

THE FOUR-LEGGED ANGEL

They say that we are a nation of animal lovers and that very often our pets often mean far more to us than some our family. Why not? In the majority of cases we can certainly rely on our pets far more than we can any human.

This was most certainly the case of Grace Johnson who had been totally blind from birth. Until recently her 'eyes' and constant companion had been Polly, a black Labrador who had been with Grace since she was a pup. Theirs was a very close and loving relationship. But, at 12 years old, Polly had been put to sleep because of an incurable growth in her stomach.

Grace was devastated, but had been extremely fortunate to get another guide dog, Buster, so quickly. Also a Labrador, he was a nice pleasant dog, but he was not Polly. Polly had known Grace's every move and, of course, poor Buster did not. It was almost as though Polly had known exactly what Grace was thinking. She had somehow been attuned to Grace's every need and had looked after her whenever she had felt unwell.

Although an animal lover and a lover of dogs in particular, Grace did not seem to have the same rapport with Buster. It did not help either that when they were out walking together in the street Buster made mistakes and hesitated in heavy traffic. Grace now had little confidence in Buster's ability to guide her safely when they were outdoors.

Grace's thoughts turned often to Polly with deep sadness. She wanted so much to love Buster in the same way, to trust him, and to look upon him with confidence as she had with Polly – but she could not.

Time passed, and the situation showed no signs of improving. When Grace was at her lowest, depressed and trying desperately to decide what to do with Buster for the best, something very strange happened.

She was on her way to the post office with Buster in the town centre when she noticed, to her surprise, that he was behaving quite calmly and doing everything just as he should. He seemed almost like a different dog, as though it was Polly – not Buster – leading her. The transformation had been so sudden that Grace was completely taken aback. When they arrived home and Grace settled herself in the armchair by the fire, Buster surprised her again by sitting close beside her, something he had never done before, usually preferring to stretch out in front of the fire.

The marked change in Buster's behaviour pleased Grace and she could suddenly feel warmth from the dog, almost as though he had really begun to care for her. In fact Buster continued to improve as the days went by and Grace and he began to develop a close, loving relationship. It was not until the local vicar called to see her that Grace realised why her dog's behaviour had changed so suddenly and dramatically.

The vicar was not aware that Polly had died and during his visit he remarked to Grace how nice it must be for her to have two dogs escorting her to the shops. Assuming that Polly was nearing her retirement age, he said how touched he was to see her training her new dog.

When Grace told him that Polly had been gone for over five months and that Buster was her new companion, the vicar simply could not believe it. He was adamant that he had seen Polly and was touched by her gentleness and concern as she walked with the new dog.

Grace continued to feel Polly's healing touch around the home for quite some time, even after Buster had learned the ropes and settled in. Thanks to Polly, Buster became Grace's trusted companion and invaluable 'eyes'.

43

AUNTY MARGARET

Although sadly no longer a ward, Mary 2, of Alder Hey Children's Hospital, used to be a veritable powerhouse of paranormal activity to me as a child.

Most of my childhood was spent in Mary 2 Ward and, although I personally experienced many ghostly happenings during some of my stays, middle-aged porter Jim had become quite accustomed to the spooky encounters.

It was 1955 and Alder Hey Hospital already had a worldwide reputation for the high standard of specialised treatment it was able to deliver, combined with the care and hospitality that it was known to extend to all its young patients.

Jim the porter had spent an extremely talkative thirty seconds with an attentive and friendly elderly man in the lift, only to find that he had vanished before they had reached the appropriate floor. In fact, this had happened to Jim several times over the years, and although he had become quite accustomed to the occasional ghostly visitor, he was never prepared for the spooky exit.

On one occasion Jim had been asked to transfer a ten year old girl to another ward, and had assumed that the young woman who accompanied them was her mother. When they arrived at the ward, Jim noticed that the young woman had gone but never thought any more about it. The following day he received a request to return to the ward, as the sister wanted to speak to him.

When Jim arrived at the sister's office and found that she was waiting for him with another woman, he began to think that he must have done something wrong.

"Jim, when you brought Sandra to the ward yesterday, was there someone else with you?" she asked, with a curious and yet serious tone to her voice.

"Yes", Jim nodded, "I thought it was the little girl's mother."

She then asked him to describe the woman, which he duly did. Upon hearing the description, the woman who was with the sister clasped her hand to her mouth.

"My God!" she gasped.

"What is it?" asked Jim. "Wasn't it the girl's mother?"

"No," answered the startled woman. "I am."

The sister tried to offer Jim an explanation for their concern.

"Sandra told her mother that her Aunt Margaret had accompanied her to the ward. We needed to make sure that it was true," explained the sister.

"There's nothing wrong with that, is there?" asked Jim, somewhat confused and keen to know exactly what the problem was.

The woman's eyes suddenly clouded with sadness as they met Jim's questioning stare, and she shook her head.

"No, not really," she said, "my sister was very fond of Sandra."

"Was?" said Jim. "Isn't she still?"

"Oh, yes. I suppose so," replied the woman. "But you see, my sister Margaret died last year."

I was frequently tended in the middle of the night by a nurse who not only looked much older than all the other nurses, but who was also dressed in a completely different way. I remember that she had a sweet fragrance surrounding her when she leaned over me at night. She always made sure that I was tucked up securely in bed and nearly always stayed with me until I fell asleep. The funny thing about it though, when my mother made enquiries about the kindly nurse, nobody seemed to know who she was.

Although I hated being away from home, Alder Hey was quite a magical place to be as a child.

Between the ages of five and seven I suppose I became much more aware of my stays in Alder Hey. The porters would sometimes transport my bed to a remote part of the hospital, where I would be placed in an empty ward by myself.

This was obviously a disused ward, with old screens and other medical equipment strewn untidily all over the floor. I would remain there all morning by myself without any food or drink, until eventually a group of student doctors would come to examine me. Why this could not be done in my own ward I shall never know. I can only say that this inflicted quite a lot of permanent emotional damage to me, and is something I have never been able to forget. To make things worse some of the windows had black shutters over them, blocking out most of the bright sunlight and making the empty ward more eerie.

On each occasion when I was taken to the empty ward, I was visited by an elderly nurse, different from the one in the previous story, wearing old fashioned clothes. She would just ask me if I was alright and her soft voice would comfort and reassure me when I was distressed. She told me her name was Rose and that she used to work on that particular ward. I saw the elderly nurse on four occasions, and the last time she came to me she explained that she was moving away and would not be able to see me again.

When the porter came to take my bed back to Mary 2 Ward, he reached over and collected some red rose petals from my pillow. 'Where did these come from?' he asked, smiling. 'Someone is looking after you?' Nurse Rose was of course a spirit, and was most probably from another time.

Billy says: Everything happened to me in Alder Hey Hospital, from being visited by spirit clowns with funny painted faces, to seeing the spirit of a child that had just died in the bed opposite mine. Although I enjoyed my sojourns in Alder Hey Hospital, I was always so happy to be discharged so that I could return home.

44

STUCK BETWEEN TWO WORLDS

It is believed that when a person dies in tragic or sudden circumstances, it often takes some time before his or her spirit fully realises that it no longer exists in the physical world.

Until the realisation comes about that the transition from the physical world has been made, the person has an awareness of two very different landscapes, one superimposed upon the other.

This divided consciousness, or state of limbo, only lasts for a very short time in a majority of cases. However, there are occasions when the deceased person subconsciously refuses to move on, so to speak, and so they still envisage themselves inhabiting a physical body that exists in a physical world. However, the only problem is that nobody in the physical world is actually able to see them.

In my work as a medium and paranormal investigator, I have experienced many such cases of so-called earthbound spirits, when I have had to use my mediumistic abilities to encourage his or her awareness to focus on the supersensual side of their existence. Once this has been achieved, the earthbound spirit 'goes home' quite peacefully, never to return to the physical world again.

This is a true story and one that involves a young man who was killed with his Jack Russell dog in a car crash.

Richard Sharp lived in a flat with his little dog, Snoop, in Livingstone Drive in the Lark Lane area of Liverpool. Although he had many friends, Richard was known to be something of a loner and spent most of the time playing with Snoop in Sefton Park. He worked for the Liverpool Parks and Gardens Department and, because he loved being outdoors, he would spend as much time as he possibly could going for walks and drives into the countryside with his four-legged friend. In fact, the two were almost inseparable and, whenever he could, Richard would even take Snoop to work with him, particularly when he was working in nearby Sefton Park.

It was July 1996 and Richard was enjoying his annual two-week summer holiday and had decided to drive out to Wales for a couple of days. He liked to paint with watercolours and had decided to take a pad and some pencils with him to make a few sketches of the picturesque countryside.

He had planned it all very carefully, just Snoop and himself and the wide-open spaces of the Welsh countryside. He was looking forward to the peace and tranquillity, which he thought the two days would bring. However, it was not meant to be.

He had only just set off on his journey, full of pleasant expectations, and had turned right from Parkfield Road into Aigburth Road, when an articulated wagon hit his little car head on after driving straight through a set of red traffic lights. Both Richard and Snoop were killed outright and his Mini was completely demolished in the impact. As is often the case, the driver of the articulated wagon escaped from the accident unhurt.

It was Richard's mother, Mrs Sharp, who contacted me through her friend. She was a staunch Catholic and so consulting mediums was contrary to her beliefs, but she was desperate. She had exhausted all other avenues and I was a last resort.

I called at her home in West Derby on Friday night, just one month exactly after her son had been killed.

"He was a lovely boy," she sighed, as she handed me his framed photograph. "Of course, he wasn't really a boy at all he was a young man. But he was still boy to me though."

She began to cry and then sat on the chair by the window overlooking the rear garden.

"He keeps coming to me," she confided, overcome with grief and confusion, "and I really don't know what to do about it."

"What do you mean?" I asked, carefully trying to coax the information from her, without upsetting her even more. "Does he come to you in your dreams?"

"Oh, yes, that too," she answered. "But he comes to me at about six every night." She drew in a deep breath and wiped the tears from her cheeks with her handkerchief. "You see Richard used to come here every night for his tea. He always had done so since leaving home when he was 18. He comes each night and sits in that chair crying to me." She indicated the chair in front of the television. "I don't know what to do. Please can you help him?"

I arranged to visit her the following evening just before 6pm. To be perfectly honest, I really thought that her son's appearance was the result of her own emotional trauma and, although I expected to 'see' something mediumistically, I was most certainly not prepared for what was going to happen.

When I arrived, Richard's mother asked me not to sit on her son's chair, as this would be where he would probably appear to us. I must say that I felt extremely nervous and was not at all sure that I would be able to help her. So I sat back in my chair and tried to relax by keeping my mind occupied in talking to her.

In the middle of our conversation, I noticed that Mrs Sharp's eyes kept moving backwards and forwards from me to the chair in front of the television. I followed her gaze and noticed a grey mist forming over the contours of the chair. It gradually became more intense and within moments I could see the faint outline of the figure of a man. I couldn't believe what my eyes were seeing and could feel my heart quickening and beads of perspiration forming across my brow. The whole process took no more than one minute and then her son was sitting on the chair facing us. He looked quite solid and I knew that I was not seeing him clairvoyantly, as Mrs Sharp could also see him.

I was not mentally prepared for the whole experience and, at this point, I must admit that I felt distinctly alarmed and all my instincts were telling me to leave, but I knew that I could not.

"Richard, love," said Mrs Sharp, gently, "I've brought someone to meet you."

I expected him to respond by turning his eyes to look in my direction, but his gaze remained fixed on his mother. He seemed to be completely oblivious to my presence and appeared to be stuck in some sort of habitual energy stream.

He began to cry and looked pleadingly at his mother.

"What's wrong with me?" he cried.

"Nothing is wrong with you, Richard," she answered in a soft, reassuring voice, her eyes looking to me for support.

"Can I help you?" I asked, as softly as I possibly could. "Please let me help you."

He ignored me completely, seemingly unaware of my presence. I realised then that I had been right in my first assumption and that he could not see me or hear me. In fact, Richard was only attuned to his mother's vibrations and so she was the only person who really had the power to help him.

He stayed in the chair for at least eight minutes, before finally disappearing in exactly the same way as he had appeared in the first place. Although this was an objective paranormal appearance, which anyone present could see, Richard himself could only be aware of his mother and the environment with which he had been so familiar in life.

That night I gave the whole experience a great deal of thought and concluded that there was no way that his mother was going to be able to help her son in the realisation and acceptance that he had, in fact, died. This was likely to be an extremely delicate process and one which had to be handled with great care and sensitivity but also with a firm and positive attitude. This, Richard's mother most definitely could not do, as she was far too emotionally involved.

After spending half the night mentally analysing the whole paranormal incident, the answer suddenly dawned on me – Snoop – Richard's dog. Next to his mother, he had been the most important living thing in his life. I knew now what had to be done. The following morning I arranged to call on Mrs Sharp again.

"As you are the only person whom he is aware of," I told her, "you are the only one who can help him."

"Just tell me what to do," she pleaded, "I will do anything to help him find peace."

"When Richard comes to you tonight, you must ask him where Snoop is," I said, hoping that the very question would encourage the dog to manifest itself. "When he becomes aware of the dog, it should persuade him to follow."

Mrs Sharp agreed and I returned to her home just before six that evening. As expected, Richard appeared before us in exactly the same way as before. Mrs Sharp hesitated at first, obviously struggling with her emotions. But then she sat bolt upright in her chair and managed to compose herself sufficiently to address her son in the way in which we had previously discussed.

"Hello, Richard, love, where is Snoop?"

At first he didn't answer and I was afraid that he wasn't going to respond to her question after all. But soon a smile beamed across his face and he repeated the dog's name, 'Snoop'. Almost immediately, Snoop appeared in front of him, seemingly unaware of our presence. The little creature wagged its tail and, without even rising from the chair; Richard disappeared along with his little canine friend. It was as simple and painless as that.

I was not convinced, at that point, that Richard would not return the following night and so I told Mrs Sharp that I would ring her at seven o'clock to make sure that everything was fine. As soon as she answered the telephone, I knew that her son had not shown up. I rang her again the following night and still there was no sign of him. Indeed, Richard never returned to his mother's home again after that night. It would seem that Snoop, his faithful canine friend, had taken him home.

45

THIRD TIME UNLUCKY

W hilst some people appear to lead charmed lives, there are others who are so unfortunate that they are said to always be in the wrong place at the wrong time.

However, even those living charmed lives can sometimes find that their luck eventually runs out, especially when they persist in tempting fate.

This true story counters the old saying that lighting does not strike in the same place twice. In fact, for John Latham it struck three times and, for him, the third time proved to be the unluckiest.

John Latham lived in Sussex Gardens, Park Road, and used to catch the number 27 bus to the junction of Smithdown Road and Lodge Lane every morning.

He worked as an engineer in nearby Chatsworth Street and so he was able to walk the short journey from Lodge Lane to his place of work in approximately ten minutes. He had made the same journey for the past twelve years and had never been late in all that time.

The first incident took place on 18 October 1951 when he was running to catch his bus home from work in Lodge Lane. As the number 27 was pulling away from the bus stop, John jumped onto the platform but lost his footing in the attempt.

He fell backwards from the bus platform and, had it not been for the quick thinking of the conductor, who caught hold of his overcoat just in time, he would have fallen to his death for sure. On this occasion he escaped with no more than a bruised forehead and extreme shock. Although badly shaken, he recovered fairly quickly and was soon able to put the whole episode to the back of his mind.

The next incident took place a few weeks later, just before Christmas, and in exactly the same place. Although he was naturally a very careful man, always mindful of the dangers encountered on icy roads, John Latham slipped again when mounting the bus in Lodge Lane.

This time, though, the conductor was not there to save him. As he fell, his overcoat belt became entangled round the handrail, causing him to fall awkwardly.

He smashed his head on the platform and was rendered unconscious. For a few moments the bus dragged him along, until the dramatic accident was brought to the attention of the driver, who managed to stop the vehicle just in time. Still unconscious, John was taken by ambulance to Sefton General Hospital, where he was kept overnight for observation.

Although his injuries were a little more extensive and severe than in the first incident, he returned to work two days later. However, the experience had forced him to confront his own mortality and he grew increasingly worried about whether there was something more sinister going on concerning his fate. His concerns were confirmed some days later.

It was New Year's Eve and once again he was rushing to catch the number 27 bus home. He mounted the bus in Lodge Lane, in exactly the same place as he always did.

As he stood on the platform, struggling to negotiate his way around the other passengers, he stumbled and a parked van caught him as he leaned back.

He was knocked from the platform of the moving bus, and within moments was dragged underneath the back wheels. His death was instantaneous and quite horrific.

There is no doubt about it, John Latham's destiny was pre-determined, and his demise was most definitely meant to take place where, how and when it did. As to whether or not he could have avoided his fate by following a different route home, we shall never know. Anyway, for John Latham it is too late!

Billy says: This story is one of five very similar cases I have collected over the years, and proved to me that some people are 'jinxed' and predestined to leave this life in a very certain way.

46

THE WEEPING LADY

Most cultures have superstitions, which have been handed down through the ages, involving harbingers of doom and disaster, like the banshee of the Irish tradition.

Such beliefs have often been greatly exaggerated and today the superstition of the banshee probably bears no resemblance to the original portentous creature.

The old weeping lady is a figure who makes an appearance in all cultures at times of great misfortune or disaster. However, just like the banshee, the appearance of the weeping lady is very often a portent of doom and disaster.

The last recorded appearances of the weeping lady in Liverpool were in 1943, once outside the Philharmonic Pub in Hardman Street and, again, in a Chinese laundry in Myrtle Street.

The Kay brothers had all joined the merchant navy together and had managed to sign up on the same ship. This was fortunate, as they had been inseparable since boyhood and carried their close bond to the extreme by marrying three sisters. John, Peter and Will had just returned from South America and were making their way to Fong's Laundry in Myrtle Street, to get some shirts cleaned for a dance on the Saturday night.

Whenever the three brothers were together, visiting town always meant calling in at several pubs along the way. Their wives reluctantly accepted this and knew only too well that any protestations would fall upon deaf ears.

Out of the three brothers, Peter had the strongest sense of adventure and always seemed to be getting himself into some sort of scrape. The other two were more cautious and quite level-headed and always had to keep an eye on their younger brother, in case he got himself into trouble.

It was Thursday afternoon and the trio had called into the Philharmonic Pub before going to the laundry further along the road. On the way into the pub, John noticed an old lady standing outside the ornate wrought iron gates, crying. She was a frail, pitiful specimen, with a woollen shawl pulled tightly around her tiny shoulders and wrinkled, aged face. Will and Peter had not noticed the women and carried on into the pub, unaware that John had stopped on the pavement outside.

He was just about to approach her, to check if she was alright, when she pointed a crooked, bony finger at him, almost accusingly and so he thought the better of it and swiftly followed his brothers inside.

"Where've you been?" asked Will, "You always disappear when it's your round."

"There's an old dear lady outside crying her eyes out," he said, sounding somewhat upset, "and I went to see if she was alright."

The three brothers soon forgot about the incident and downed a few pints before continuing on their way towards the Chinese laundry in Myrtle Street. As they entered the steam-filled shop, which was owned by the brothers' friend, John noticed the same old women coming out. She was still crying bitterly and he stood watching her, as she progressed slowly down Myrtle Street, away from the city centre. Will came out to see where his brother John was, whilst Peter stayed inside chatting to his friend, Li Fong.

"What's the matter with her?" asked Will. "Is she alright?"

"Don't know!" John answered. "That's the women I saw before standing outside the Philharmonic. She's still crying."

As they watched the old women walking down the street she stopped and turned to face the two brothers, then pointed to Will, again, almost accusingly. John looked at Will and frowned.

"She did that to me before!" he said. "She's obviously not all there." Will laughed as they both turned and went back inside the laundry.

Later on that day, as the three brothers were making their way through the town and were just about to catch a bus home, Will saw the old woman again standing outside of the Adelphi Hotel, still crying. He nudged John as they passed her by but, again, Peter was occupied elsewhere and had not noticed her.

The following evening the three brothers decided to take their wives out for a drink and then afterwards into town for a meal. They visited quite a few pubs throughout the evening, but decided to remain in the Willow Bank, in Smithdown Road, until last orders were called.

The pub was crowded and, by 10pm, everyone in the snug was singing. By the time the three brothers and their wives had left the pub, John, Will and Peter were quite drunk and had to be supported. Peter, as usual, was playing the fool and was trying to walk along the small wall outside the building next to the pub. Unable to keep his balance, he fell awkwardly onto the pavement smashing his head on the wall as he tumbled. He was taken to nearby Sefton General Hospital, where he was kept in for observation.

Over the following few days, the brothers received word that they had to join their ship, The Western Star, in Ireland, from where they would carry cargo to South America. Because of the accident, Peter was unable to travel and this would be the first time that the brothers had been separated. As Peter had suffered a fairly serious concussion during the fall, he had to spend at least another week in hospital. John and Will said their farewells to him and left early the following morning for Ireland.

A week later Peter was discharged from hospital. He was extremely impatient to be reunited with his brothers and could not wait for them to return. He knew that they would be away for at least eight weeks and so he arranged a family party for their return. However, on the Friday after Peter was discharged from hospital, the wives of John and Will received some appalling news. Their ship had been torpedoed and there were no survivors.

Peter was devastated and overwhelmed with irrational feelings of guilt. He felt that he should have been with them and was somehow convinced that he had let his brothers down. Although he had not actually seen the old woman, Peter remembered his brothers talking about her. He knew now that she was the fabled weeping woman, the legendary harbinger of death, known to point an accusing finger at those who were about to die tragically. If only John and Will had known, thought Peter, they would not have pitied her then.

Billy says: This is a true story and one that circulated during both the First and Second World Wars.
There were many victims of the Weeping Lady, also known as the Pointing Lady, and I actually got this story from Pete himself.

47

To Where the Narrow Road Forks

When John and Pat Rafferty first viewed the Victorian house in Ullet Road, they fell in love with it almost immediately. John's new job, with a firm in Edge Lane, had necessitated the move from Manchester to Liverpool.

They were presently staying with Pat's parents in Childwall until they had found somewhere permanent of their own. With two children already and now another one on the way, they needed a bigger house than the one they had sold in Manchester and they both agreed that 33 Ullet Road was perfect for their expanding family. It was 1950 and Liverpool had not yet recovered from the War. John had been promoted to a new position, which meant more money and far better prospects. Their baby was due in three months time, on 15 September, so it was extremely important that they found a house quickly.

They had managed to save quite a bit of money over the years and they borrowed the rest from the bank. John's only vice was an occasional flutter on the horses. He had always been quite lucky and had won over a thousand pounds just before they had moved from Manchester. They bought the house in Ullet Road and moved in within six weeks. Although the décor was not to their liking, the house itself was exactly what they had both wanted. The area was quite respectable and the large gardens back and front made it ideal for the children.

The whole family settled down very quickly in their new home and Pat gave birth to a little girl on 14 September, making the family complete.

When John came in from work one cold November night, he announced to Pat that he had to go to a farewell dinner for a work colleague, who was retiring at the end of the year.

"It's on the 18th of December," he told her. "It's being held at a hotel in Ormskirk and, unfortunately, it's for men only, so I'm afraid you can't come. I'm not looking forward to it, but there's absolutely no way I can get out of it!"

The 18 December was a cold and frosty day with a threat of thick fog in the evening, according to the weather forecast. Although Ormskirk was not very far away, John was not looking forward to driving in such hazardous conditions, especially by himself. Although it was foggy by 4pm, it was not as bad as the weatherman had predicted and John had come home early from work so that he could take his time driving to Ormskirk. He was not really familiar with the route and so he wanted to leave in good time, just in case the weather got worse.

It took him over an hour to reach Ormskirk, by which time the fog was extremely thick and he could scarcely see the bonnet of the car, let alone the road in front of him. The headlights cast a feeble beam and only sufficed to reveal the thick, impenetrable grey fog all around him. He drove with his face as close to the windscreen as possible and he had reduced his speed to 10 miles an hour. The concentration required made him feel hot and flustered and he undid his tie with a sigh of relief. He could never stand anything tight around his neck anyway.

It was impossible to see any road signs or landmarks and he did not have a clue where he was, or even if he was still actually driving on the road at all. Pat's last words kept passing annoyingly through his mind: "Only a fool would go out on a night like this." She had warned him and he had to admit that she was right. He was a fool and now he regretted not having made some excuse not to go. After all, he hardly knew Ted Jones and had only spoken to him on three occasions in all the time they had worked together.

Stopping the car at what he had estimated was the roadside; John got out to get his bearings and to see if there was anyone passing by who could tell him where exactly he was.

Not surprisingly, there was absolutely no one around on such a night, but he had an idea that he was in the middle of the countryside. He thought he could hear cows some yards away and there was the familiar damp odour of farmland in winter, intermingled with the smell of fog.

By now, John had resigned himself to the obvious fact that he was not going to make it to the function and he just wanted to be back home with his wife and children, in front of the warm fire or, better still, tucked up in bed.

Instead he was stuck in thick fog, in the middle of nowhere with no clue about his exact position. He decided to drive a little further on and, if necessary, he would sleep in the car until the fog had lifted or even, perhaps, stay the night at a country inn, if he was fortunate enough to come across one.

He had driven for no more than five minutes when he reached a spot where the fog appeared to be a little thinner. He could just about distinguish the narrow road he was driving along and noticed that he had reached a fork. Pausing for a moment, he decided almost immediately to take the right fork in the road and somehow had a strange feeling that he knew exactly where he was going, as though he had been there before, even though he knew this was not the case.

Eventually he found himself parked at the gates of what looked like an old manor house and, as the gates had been left open, he decided to drive through them and along the winding driveway until the old house itself was reached. From the very moment that he had reached the fork in the road, he had been overwhelmed by feelings that he could only describe as déjà vu.

Now the old manor house itself seemed uncannily familiar to him, even though he had never visited this part of the country before. As he climbed wearily from his car, he seemed to have a sense of 'knowing' exactly where he was. Even the five stone steps up to the ornately carved oak doors seemed so familiar and, for a moment, his thoughts drifted back to the days when the house was first built. He had always had an affinity with the historical period during which the house had been built and nurtured a strong desire to collect pieces of furniture from that time.

Pat, however, had more modern tastes and despised anything that was older than she was, so she had never been able to indulge in his passion.

John had intended to ask the people who lived in the house for some assistance, or perhaps they would allow him to stay there, at least until the fog had lifted sufficiently for him to resume his journey. As he ascended the stone steps, he could see that the old place was in darkness and was probably unlived in.

He reached out for the heavy metal knocker and the door opened, with no more than a little shove. As he entered the hallway, he was immediately overwhelmed by the musty smells and cold, damp atmosphere associated with empty houses and he quickly surmised that nobody had lived there for quite some time.

Before venturing further into the house, he called out to make quite certain that it was empty. His voice echoed through the darkness of the empty house and, although the old place was eerie, he did not feel uncomfortable or afraid in any way whatsoever.

He found an old oil lamp that still contained a small amount of oil and, after several attempts, he managed to light it. All the time he seemed to be guided by some deep-rooted instinct, as he systematically wended his way through the empty house from room to room.

He seemed to be quite familiar with the architectural layout and was quite surprised to discover that he knew exactly where the kitchen was situated. He could not understand why the old house was so familiar to him, or why he was experiencing a strange feeling of excitement in the pit of his stomach. He was so preoccupied with the search that he had quite forgotten the reason why he was there in the first place.

Unperturbed by his surroundings, he decided that he would find a comfortable chair in which to settle down for the night.

Although the old manor had obviously been empty for some time, all the furniture was still in place, covered with white, protective dustsheets. John snuggled down on a large, plush settee and, in no time at all had fallen fast asleep.

He woke up just before six o'clock in the morning and, although it was still fairly dark outside, he could see the moon shining through the window at the top of the stairs and therefore knew that the fog had cleared. His night spent in the unheated house had left him feeling stiff and chilled and he could not wait to get home. Pat would be worried sick and he would have to find a telephone box as soon as possible to let her know that he was alright.

The silvery light of the moon illuminated the room and he could now see the fireplace quite clearly. Its ornate surround was engraved with a family crest and the name, John Barrington Moore, was etched into its centre. John went cold as he read the name. It was so familiar and seemed to jog some ancient memory within him. His mind was flooded with images and thoughts of days gone by. He was sure that he had read somewhere that John Barrington Moore had been hanged for murder in the nineteenth century. He could not quite remember where exactly he had read it, but he definitely, somehow, recalled the name. This made him feel quite unsettled and he wanted to leave at once.

As soon as John was seated in his car and had started the engine, he could feel his heart pounding inside his chest. He turned the vehicle round in front of the house and accelerated quickly down the gravel driveway glancing nervously in the mirror as he sped through the gates, leaving the imposing old house behind him. The whole episode occupied his mind to such an extent on the way home that he completely forgot to phone Pat to let her know that he was safe and well.

John's stay in the old house was the sole topic of conversation for over a week and he knew that his wife did not believe a word of his story. And so, on a bright Sunday afternoon, two weeks after the New Year, he decided to take a drive with her and the children to find the old house.

It was a beautiful clear day and, to John's great surprise, he was able to drive straight to it, without getting lost once.

He drove through the gates and along the winding driveway towards the front entrance, with a rush of excitement quickening his heart. He was looking forward to seeing the imposing edifice once again, this time in full daylight and he wanted to prove to Pat, once and for all, that he had been telling the truth. But he was in for a nasty shock.

As the car emerged from the driveway and edged towards the front of the house, he could not believe what he was seeing. Before him was only a shell of a house, silhouetted against the clear blur sky; its fire charred walls now decaying beneath the winds of time.

"Some house!" scoffed Pat sarcastically. "And I suppose you're now going to tell me that this is not the place?"

John pulled the car to a halt and just sat in stunned silence, unable to respond to his wife's remark. Then somebody tapped on the side window and he turned his head to see an elderly man standing there smiling at him.

"Nice to see you again, Mr Barrington," the man grinned, with a sudden look of embarrassment as John turned to face him. "Oh! I do beg your pardon, sir," he said, "I thought you were Mr Barrington Moore."

John felt an icy shiver pass right through him, as though someone had walked across his grave. He climbed out of the car, eager to speak to the man.

"I'm the gardener here, sir," he said, "I've been looking after these gardens since I was a young man."

"The house…" John stammered. "What's happened to the house?"

"Oh, the house was burnt down in the late 19th century," the old man answered.

John went even colder and could not believe the information he had just been given. He knew that he had stayed there on that foggy night and had looked around the old house and seen the fireplace with the inscription on its surround.

"That's not possible!" he replied, in a daze. "I came here..."

He stopped suddenly to face the old house and the old man noticed the puzzled look on his face.

"John Barrington Moore murdered his uncle in a fit of rage," explained the old man. "He then set fire to the house. He was hanged six months later." The man paused for a moment, while John absorbed the information. But he had known that already. He had remembered it when he was looking at the fireplace. "You're the spitting image of the present Mr John Barrington Moore. The spitting image you are," the gardener went on.

John found the whole thing a little too bizarre to take in. He felt unable to tell Pat the whole incredible story, because he knew she would not believe a word of it.

"What was the name of the uncle who was murdered?" he asked.

"Charles Barrington Moore. He was quite wealthy and lived in this house which was owned by his nephew."

John was fascinated and wanted to find out all he could about the family.

"Why did he murder his uncle?"

"He threatened to cut his nephew out of his will," continued the old man. "John Barrington Moore was a gambling man and had lost all his money. He burned the house down to cover his misdeeds."

The old gardener bade John farewell and made his way slowly back along the path towards the gardens at the rear of the house. John stood there for a moment, pensively watching the retreating figure. It was all coming back to him, image after powerful image, flooding his mind with memories that he was now somehow being forced to remember.

John never believed in reincarnation, but this was all too much of a coincidence. He was being overwhelmed by strong emotions from the past and for the moment he felt as though he was living in two completely different ages.

"I am John Barrington Moore!" he muttered to himself. "I have returned..."

His thoughts were sharply interrupted by Pat, who was calling him from the car.

"John, can we go now, the kids are starving and the baby's waking up!"

He climbed back into the car with a heavy sigh. He started the engine and turned the car in front of the house for the last time, before accelerating quickly down the long driveway and through the gates, without glancing back once.

He was now certain that he was John Barrington Moore and that, for some reason, he had returned to the house, which he had destroyed. John never returned to the house, for he had no desire to be hanged for the same crime twice!

Billy says: This is yet another case for reincarnation, and a story that was related to me some years ago by John himself. He told me that the experience had changed his whole life, and certainly made him look more closely at himself and the possibility that he had lived before.

48

THE GHOST OF MRS SIMCOCK

A melancholy catastrophe' was the way in which the Gore's General Advertiser, on Thursday 28 August 1817, described the death of Mrs Simcock in Trentham Street, Salthouse Dock in Liverpool.

The woman had an infant in her arms when she was thrown down by the leading horse of a cart, laden with flour, on its way to a warehouse on the cobbled road. The poor woman, with no regard for her own safety, tried desperately to save her small baby girl who clung desperately to her mother.

The wheels of the heavy cart went over the woman's legs and thighs and, although her child received only minor abrasions, Mrs Simcock died of her injuries in the Liverpool Infirmary in the early hours of Monday morning.

On the following Tuesday, a coroner's inquest was held and a verdict of manslaughter was returned against the carter, saying that he was 'negligent' and greatly at fault. He was thus committed to Lancaster Castle for trial at the assizes, on 27 August 1817. The woman's child completely recovered.

The deceased woman was the wife of trader Thomas Simcock of Hurst Street, Liverpool. His wife's death devastated him and it is said that he never recovered from the traumatic ordeal.

The ghost of Mrs Simcock has been seen in exactly the same place that she was killed on that dreaded rainy night where Trentham Street was situated by the Salthouse Dock.

Although Mrs Simcock's daughter was not killed in the awful accident, witnesses claimed to have heard a woman's distress and a young child crying, always on Friday 22 August around 6pm.

Billy says: As far as I can find, Trentham Street is no longer there and I can only surmise that it is now called by another name. The fact that Mrs Simcock's daughter was not killed and yet her ghostly cries can still be heard, suggests that it is the usual 'paranormal memory replay', a sort of photographic image of the event, caught in the atmosphere, like a picture in the wind...

49

The Ghostly Goings on at St George's Hall

In the winter of 1998, I was invited by Peter Grant of the Liverpool Echo to take part in a charity 'Ghost Watch' at St George's Hall.

Thinking that it was going to be one of the usual journalistically hyped events, I must say I went along not really expecting anything significant to happen, and thought that I would back home and tucked up in bed by midnight – Wrong!

St George's Hall is steeped in history, and its courtroom has sent many a murderous villain to the gallows. Because St George's Hall has a great deal of history attached to it, I was looking forward to at least exploring this magnificent edifice and taking the opportunity to look at the beautiful architecture.

The so-called 'Ghost Watch' began in the cells, deep in the bowels of the building, and I was immediately drawn to one particular cell. I asked to be left alone for ten minutes to see if I could actually 'feel' anything, and I was surprised when I saw the diminutive form of an old Victorian lady with a very dirty face and wearing shabby work clothes.

After a while I received communication from the old woman, who explained that she was a coal merchant in Victorian times. Although in the beginning my communication with her was somewhat incoherent and slightly confused, the longer I remained in the cell alone she became much stronger and very clear.

She eventually told me that she had been attacked by two young thugs, who had been surprised by her strength when she beat them to death with a coal shovel. The old woman who became known as 'Black Kate' was hanged for her crime – a great injustice, when she, after all, was only protecting herself.

Midnight came and went, and the longer I remained in the building the more I could feel. I began to feel quite excited and my friend Peter Grant and myself began to enjoy what looked like being an eventful evening.

Wending our way along the maze of corridors, I could feel myself almost being transported back through time, and gradually became psychically aware of many different personalities from various periods of history. One frightening figure was that of a veritable giant of a man whose thick Irish accent boomed at me from one of the cells. He was a serial offender primarily there to have somewhere to bed for the night. He explained that the local constabulary got quite used to him and would ignore his crimes.

Realising this, he decided to do something more serious, and so beat a drinking partner to death. Due to Shamus Riley being mentally challenged, he wrongly assumed that he would simply be sent to prison for life. The huge Irish man was sentenced to death in April 1870 and was hanged at Walton in the same year (rough justice, Shamus! That'll teach you).

The door of the cell Shamus Riley was kept in whilst awaiting his trial slammed closed by itself and a pungent smell pervaded the tiny little space. Apparently, the Irish man was known to be in the habit of always breaking wind when he was in the cell with someone else. He did this in his mischievous attempt to have them removed so that he could be in the cell alone.

Our ghostly sojourn at St George's Hall was really a lot more interesting than I originally thought it would be, and we called it a night just after 3am. I am planning to return to St George's Hall sometime in the near future, and this time I will take some of my scientific equipment with me, in the hope of proving once and for all that St George's Hall really does have a supernatural as well as a historical side.

50

GHOSTS OF WAVERTREE

It's funny that certain stories we are told when we are children somehow stay with us forever. One such story that my father and a neighbour told me when I was about six years old, concerns the impressive old mansion set back on Church Road on the corner, which is today the Royal School for the Blind.

The story was about the daughter of the owner of the house, some time in the mid 1800s, who had fallen in love with the family's coachman, Edward Lawton. The girl's father was understandably unhappy about the liaison and threatened to disinherit his daughter if she did not end the relationship immediately.

Ignoring her father's wishes she decided to elope with Edward Lawton and had arranged to meet him at one of the gates leading to the house. As the coach man had been delayed in the house the young girl was waiting patiently for him at the gate alone. Upon reading the brief note his daughter had left for him, the girl's father immediately went after her in a coach and, unaware that she was still waiting for her lover at the gate, accidentally ran her down and killed her.

The distraught father allegedly swore that the gates would be sealed and remain closed forever. My father went on to tell me that the young woman's ghost frequently appears at the gate where she was to meet her lover, and that she always appears tearful and quite distressed.

However, there are a few discrepancies in the ghostly saga. For one, the actual gate is far too narrow for a coach to pass through it unless, of course, the girl's father was on a horse which is the more likely story. The other discrepancy is that the original ornamental gates were in fact removed in 1955 when they rusted away and, although historical records do substantiate the 'eloping' claim, there is no evidence to suggest that the father killed his daughter at all, but simply wanted the gates sealed forever to remind him of what his daughter had done.

THE CURSE OF THE OLD WINDMILL

At the far end of Charles Berrington Road in Wavertree, there are the foundations of a 15th century windmill that once overlooked a quarry – remnants of a bygone age.

Before the windmill was demolished in 1916, its rotating sails were secured so that they would cast a shadow of a cross onto the surrounding ground in a feeble attempt to rid the area of a curse many believed had been placed upon it by an evil spirit living in the quarry. Residents in the area believed that several people killed there had fallen prey to the evil curse and as a result, numerous attempts were made to exorcise the evil force that allegedly pervaded the whole area. When all attempts to rid the cursed location of the evil spirit had failed, the quarry was eventually filled in and for a while all was silent and nothing eventful occurred for some years.

Over the last thirty years residents in the area have heard the ghostly cries of a young girl in the dead of night, coming from the direction of where the windmill used to stand. The ghostly apparition of a young girl with long hair has also been seen playing in the area and witnesses have claimed that she simply disappears when anyone approaches her.

In the late eighteenth century, 11-year-old Margaret Coots was playing with her brother and friends by the windmill on a blustery March afternoon, when her hair allegedly became entangled in the rotating blades of the windmill and her neck was broken as she was pulled up by the circular motion of the mechanism.

James Grimshaw is said to have worked at the mill and was killed when a heavy bale fell on him. Several weeks later his son was also killed at the mill, in exactly the same way.

Although the ghostly appearance of the little girl is the one most frequently reported, in the mid 1940s witnesses claimed to have see an old lady wearing a black shawl and smoking a long white clay pipe. She became known as 'the smoking lady'.

51

The Wedding Ring

Eileen Chapman was having a well-needed cup of coffee with her daughter, Christine, in Capaldi's Café on Smithdown Road. They'd just spent a couple of enjoyable hours rummaging through tables of junk at a jumble sale in nearby St Agnes's Church Hall and were inspecting the contents of a jewellery box Eileen had bought.

Although the box contained nothing of any value, it was the jewellery box itself that had caught Eileen's eye. It was a beautifully crafted ornamental piece and at least 70 years old, thought Eileen, who always had a keen eye for a bargain. As her daughter emptied the rest of the contents of the box onto the table, she noticed a small envelope tucked into one of the pockets of the satin lining.

It contained a lady's wedding ring, engraved with the initials M.B. and the date 7.8.23. As they sat sipping their coffee and discussing the ring, Frank Burrows an elderly neighbour of Eileen's walked into the café. "Thank God I found you," said the elderly gentleman, with a look of relief on his face. "I was told you were here."

"What is it?" asked Eileen, with concern, thinking that her husband, John, had had an accident or something. "Sit down. What's wrong?"

The look of relief on the man's face immediately put Eileen at ease and his eyes settled on the jewellery box sitting on the table.

"Mavis from the church told me you'd bought my wife's jewellery box," he began. "When I gave it to them I'd forgotten that I'd put her wedding ring in it for safe keeping. I hadn't intended to give the ring as well."

Eileen laughed and retrieved the ring from the box. "That's alright," she said affectionately, handing it to him. "I wondered whose ring it was. It's a good job it was me who bought it and not a total stranger. You'd never have seen the ring again."

The old man thanked Eileen and, placing the ring securely in his pocket, he left the café.

"What a coincidence," remarked Eileen. "He was very lucky it was me who bought it. His wife Mary only died last year and he's so lost without her."

Later, as Eileen and her daughter walked down Dovedale Road towards their home at the far end by Queens Drive, they saw an ambulance and a police car outside of Frank Burrows' house.

Eileen's husband, John, was standing on the step talking to the lady who had been looking after Frank since his wife Mary had died.

"What's happened?" asked Eileen. "Is Frank alright?"

"Unfortunately not!" replied her husband. "It looks as though he had a massive heart attack, most probably in the night."

"That's not possible," retorted Eileen, astonished. "He was talking to us in Capaldi's only a short while ago." She nervously checked her watch. "Yes, no more than an hour ago." She looked at her daughter for confirmation and she agreed.

"That's not possible," said the woman, solemnly. "I found him around midday." She paused for a moment. "He was clutching his wife's wedding ring in his hand." Eileen went cold as the woman retrieved the ring from her handbag and showed it to her. "I kept it for safe keeping."

Eileen and her daughter were speechless and just looked at each other, totally shocked. Frank Burrows had come to Eileen after he had died to ask for his wife's wedding ring back. And now thanks to her he was at peace.

52

STRANGE GHOSTLY SIGHTINGS OF JOHN LENNON

U sually when I'm in company and it's discovered that I am a medium, there's always one person who will either ask if I get any vibes from them or they want to tell me about their own experiences.

Although this is sometimes annoying, I always have to be polite and at least pretend that I am interested. The first of these two stories took place some years ago when I was giving an after-dinner talk in The Scarisbrick Hotel in Southport to a retired ladies' guild. The meal had been eaten and the talk had been given and I was just about to discreetly leave before I became someone's captive audience, as is always the case in these events. I was making my way through the door when I was stopped by a well-spoken woman in her late sixties. "Do you mind if I have a quiet word?" she said politely. After checking the time on my watch, I led the lady to a quiet corner.

"What is it?" I asked, thinking that she was going to produce a ring belonging to her dead husband to see if I could pick anything up from it. However, I was wrong and completely taken aback by what she told me.

"I hope you don't think I'm loopy," she said, grinning nervously. "But I just wanted to see what you thought." The woman paused for a moment, and then added, "neither myself nor my husband has ever believed in the supernatural or ghosts."

I could tell that she looked quite serious and eager to tell me her story, and so I reassured her as best as I could and this is exactly what she told me.

Doris Berryton lived in Woolton with her husband Will and their mongrel Butch. They had both been retired for some years and frequently took their dog for a walk up by the now famous Strawberry Field, one of their favourite locations.

One clear November afternoon, the couple had parked their car and were walking towards the gates to Strawberry Field, when they noticed a woman and a young man standing there just staring over the gate.

The woman was in her seventies and the young man in his thirties, quite tall and slim with shoulder-length mousy-coloured hair and wearing gold-rimmed spectacles.

When they had reached the couple the woman turned and smiled. "Isn't it a lovely day?" she said to Doris, smiling. "It's lovely this time of the year. My nephew and I love Strawberry Field."

Doris agreed and after they had exchanged a few pleasantries, her husband engaged in conversation with the woman about the history of Strawberry Field.

Whilst the friendly chit-chat was taking place, Doris couldn't help but notice that the young man looked so familiar, and she just couldn't help staring at him.

"Nice dog," the young man smiled, stooping to stroke Butch. As he did Butch moved quickly away from his hand. "Doesn't like me," he laughed, standing up straight again and grinning.

It suddenly dawned on Doris who the young man looked like, and she had felt so silly for staring at him.

"Of course," she laughed, almost apologetically, "you look like John Lennon." The young man didn't comment on what Doris had said, but just threw back his shoulders and grinned almost knowingly.

Doris managed to pull her husband away from the woman and they had walked no more than ten yards from where they had been standing talking, when they both looked back and were shocked to see that the young man and the woman had gone! They'd both disappeared completely. The road was deserted.

As far as I could see this story was true. John Lennon and his aunt Mimi used to visit the summer fete at Strawberry Field every year, and it is said that John used to be so excited when he heard the band begin to play.

Strawberry Field was a Salvation Army Orphanage until it closed in 2005. It is still visited by Beatles fans from all over the world. Although Yoko will not divulge the location where John Lennon's ashes have been scattered, some people believe that they may have been buried at Strawberry Field, one of John's favourite Liverpool locations.

NO 9 NEWCASTLE ROAD

John Lennon also had family connections with Newcastle Road, and even named one of his songs after it – Number 9 Dream featured on the Beatle's White Album.

Shortly after John Lennon's death I was living in Charles Berrington Road, adjacent from Newcastle Road where John had lived at some point in his life. He was believed to have had some happy memories of 9 Newcastle Road, which is why he penned the song.

Although as a medium I am frequently told some quite ridiculous stories, I decided to share these with you because they were consistent and made sense. I think John Lennon had only been dead for about 18 months when 77-year-old Mrs Ann Maloney dropped her shopping more or less outside of number 9 Newcastle Road and was helped by a young man with shoulder-length hair, a beard and wearing round gold rimmed spectacles. It was just before 5pm and she was on her way towards her home in nearby Heathfield Road. Ann felt so embarrassed when her plastic shopping bag ripped open and tins of beans and frozen peas fell on the pavement. At first she did not look at the young man, but once all her bits of shopping had been collected and she had transferred them to another bag, she turned to thank him. At that moment she was overcome with a strange feeling and although her good Samaritan looked so familiar to her, her memory was not as good as it used to be and she just thought that maybe he was a neighbour's son. She thanked him for helping her, and the politely made an attempt to recall his name. "Aren't you ..." she stuttered, prompting him to say his name.

"I'm John," he grinned, turning to walk from where she was heading. Ann was still none the wiser, and turned to looked back at the young man – but he had gone – disappeared completely. Before she had reached the end of Newcastle Road she stopped in her tracks. "Of course!" she blurted. "It was John Lennon!"

A similar sighting was made around the same time of day three weeks later. However, this time the person involved in the ghostly confrontation was 24-year-old trainee solicitor Pamela McCallister, an enthusiastic Beatles fan. She allegedly came face to face with John Lennon when she turned the corner to make her way down Newcastle Road. This time though he was accompanied by an elderly lady who the young woman claimed was John's aunt Mimi. As on previous sightings the two disappeared completely from sight.

The interesting thing about the ghostly sightings of John Lennon was the way he appeared to the eye witnesses, with long hair and even on one occasion with a beard.

When he was actually murdered he had very short hair and no beard. In fact, a spirit will very often choose to appear when they think they looked their best. And they may even look completely different on each ghostly appearance.

53

THE GHOST OF MRS RIMMER

The brutal murder of Mrs Rimmer of Cramborne Road in Wavertree shocked the little community in 1951. Although the perpetrators of the most vicious and callous act, Devlin and Burns, were caught and ultimately hanged for their crime, the horrific death of this very inoffensive middle-aged lady still casts a shadow over the Wavertree community today.

She was bludgeoned to death behind her own front door and was discovered by her son the following day. Mrs Rimmer's untimely death contributed to Wavertree's infamous titles of 'Murder Mile' and caused all those living in the area to be extra vigilant.

I was five years old when this shocking murder took place and have vague recollections of the police conducting a spot check on all the cars travelling along Lawrence Road and other main traffic routes in the area. I had grown up in Wavertree and knew Cramborne Road extremely well. In my profession as a medium and paranormal investigator, I was naturally interested in the house where Mrs Rimmer was actually murdered and wondered whether or not the current residents had experienced anything of a supernatural nature as a result.

However, it was only a few years ago now when I was formatting the programmes for my new Channel One Television series, that I had decided to include Mrs Rimmer's murder in the programme. Not knowing the name of the person who now lives there,

I decided to call at the house, rather than sending a letter. The new occupant had only been living there for four years and, to my surprise, she was not aware of anything untoward ever having taken place in her home. She invited me into the hallway and I told her the full story of the murder and asked if she had ever experienced anything of a paranormal nature.

At first she told me that she had not, but then said that she remembered a strange occurence when she had first moved in to the house, on 19 August. On her first night there she was woken up by a loud crashing sound coming from downstairs. When she investigated the noise, she saw that the mirror on the wall in the hallway right by the front door had mysteriously fallen onto the floor, without breaking. Mrs Rimmer was actually murdered in the hallway on 18 August. In fact, her body was not found until the following day, 19 August, which makes the noise quite significant.

Furthermore, whilst I stood in the hallway listening to the lady's story, I suddenly felt a sharp, biting chill pass over me, as though someone had opened a door somewhere in the house. The previously warm and pleasant feeling that had pervaded the house was suddenly transformed into a cold, disturbing one. Although I was fairly certain that Mrs Rimmer had long since gone from the house, the full force of her distress on the night she was brutally murdered was still there and I could feel it.

When someone dies under such brutal circumstances, there is an incredible release of emotion which somehow infiltrates the psychic structure of the building in which the incident took place. This vibrant force impregnates the subtle atmosphere of the bricks and mortar, thus integrating with the paranormal nature of the house as a whole.

The phenomena produced under such circumstances are often perpetuated by the fear created in the minds of all those who come within the confines of the building. Paranormal activity is extremely insidious and can insinuate itself into the auric field of a person quite quickly.

Fear is often the greatest enemy when confronted with a paranormal problem and once the mind is thrown into the fear/adrenalin cycle, the person's resistance is immediately lowered.

In fact, in the majority of cases there is very often no certain way to eradicate paranormal disturbance once it has been well and truly established. Nor is demolition of the haunted property an answer to the problem, for this merely destroys the physical structure of the building, leaving the subtle matter completely untouched.

However, there are occasions when refurbishment or even redecoration can aid the process of 'clearing' the paranormal disturbance from a house.

54

THE GHOSTS OF PARKLEA MANOR

I have lived in Liverpool most of my life and had no idea that there was such a place as Fulwood Park, a private secluded road lined with houses that were once inhabited by wealthy merchants, writers, solicitors and even slave traders.

As you turn right from Sefton Park into Aigburth Road and drive along a few hundred yards before turning left through the once very impressive gates into the quiet, leafy suburban road, you are immediately transported back into the early part of the 19th century. But sadly, the now dilapidated Victorian architecture is a grim reminder of the opulence of those days when Liverpool was a thriving port and the wealthy frequently lived within the confines of their own self-created communities.

Once in Fulwood Park the road meanders for a short distance before reaching the gates of Parklea Manor, allegedly the most haunted house in Liverpool.

Even though the original ornate gates along with their cast iron railings have long since gone, it does not require much imagination to see that the cracked and decaying walls of the old manor house once represented the finest architecture and wealth of those bygone Victorian days.

Although now in a sorry state, walking through the double oak doors into the spacious hallway, with its black and white mosaic marble floor, one is immediately overwhelmed with a sense of being watched by many disembodied eyes.

Parklea Manor was once the home of Margaret Blackler, the heir to the Blackler fortune and owner of the well-known department store, situated on the corner of Elliot Street and Great Charlotte Street in Liverpool city centre.

The ghost of Margaret Blackler is frequently seen wandering along the maze of corridors and sometimes descending the broad staircase to the library below. Lady Margaret Blackler had no children and died in Parklea Manor in 1957. Now it would seem she simply refuses to vacate her home.

Apart from the ghost of Margaret Blackler, the sound of a ghostly brass band is occasionally heard in the now derelict ballroom on the west wing of the old house and women in long flowing gowns are seen making their way merrily down the broad staircase to the wood-panelled drawing room at the front of the building. The owner of the house was frequently woken in the dead of night to the sound of disembodied voices of young women giggling and chatting on the landing outside her bedroom. And clouds of cigar smoke would often be seen spiralling above an old Chesterfield chair in the study, even though no one in the house smoked.

The ghost of Lady Margaret Blackler would frequently be seen standing at the top of the broad staircase, staring with some displeasure at whoever was walking up the stairs towards her.

Many different types of phenomena were said to have occurred in Parklea Manor in Fulwood Park and, on one occasion a ring belonging to the owner's mother went missing. They looked everywhere for the piece of sentimental jewellery to no avail, and found it six months later on the floor of a derelict room that had been locked up for many years. Ghostly mischievous hands were in fact responsible for many things going missing, from a slipper to a porcelain ornament that was seemingly dematerialised from its resting place on the mantel in the kitchen and then found lying by itself in the dark and dismal cellar.

As with many old manor houses, the servant's bells are just some of the Victorian fixtures that still remain, forming an integral part of the house's original character. It would seem that even from the grave, Lady Blackler still demands service as her bell regularly echoes between the empty spaces of the old kitchen, never failing to send an icy chill through the entire household.

A day does not go by without some ghostly goings on at Parklea Manor. Even those who come to stay have been disturbed when a disembodied hand brushes through their hair, or a woman's face has looked out at them from the old mirror on the landing.

I have been to Parklea Manor many times and have never failed to 'see' or 'hear' something of a paranormal nature. On one occasion I thought a neighbour's child had wandered cheekily through the open front door, only to discover that the little girl in a long white frilly dress had disappeared at the end of the hallway.

Parklea Manor was built in 1840 and there are horrible rumours – and some evidence in the cellars – that black slaves were actually kept prisoner there, having been brought along narrow tunnels from ships docked in the nearby River Mersey. The chains and shackles are still there in the damp and very dark cellars, shameful and grim reminders that slave trafficking was once one of the most lucrative trades in the world.

A ghostly cacophony of men's distressed voices is often heard echoing along the dark tunnels leading to the cellars of Parklea Manor and the cracking of a whip and clanking of chains pierce the cold and heavy air. Even in the intense heat of the summer a strange chill can be felt through the cellars of the old house, and the ghosts of times long since gone still linger in the shadows.

Today Parklea Manor has been sold to developers and will shortly be refurbished and developed into luxury apartments. Although the once geometrically landscaped gardens are now overgrown, they too will shortly be subjected to the developer's bulldozer and transformed once again.

Billy says: I wonder what Lady Margaret Blackler would think? From what I have heard of the ghostly goings on at Parklea Manor, I am quite sure that Lady Margaret at least will only see the house as it always has been to her – her home and the place she obviously loved.

55

The Ghostly Errand Boy of the Daily Post and Echo

Jimmy Green Teeth, as he was known locally, had always been a regular visitor to my house every Sunday morning. As far as I knew he just came to deliver comics for me and the previous day's newspapers for my parents.

In fact, I had grown up with this inoffensive bespectacled elderly man, who always wore a flat cap and long overcoat. Although everyone called him Jimmy Green Teeth, I knew him as 'Andy' and never asked my parents why.

Andy had always been there from the very beginning of my life and so I always felt safe with him. It was only when I was about seven years old that I was told that Andy used to work as a sort of errand boy at the Liverpool Daily Post and Echo, when its main depot was in Victoria Street right in Liverpool city centre. Andy was mentally challenged and always joked that his disability had been a prerequisite for working for this particular newspaper. Of course, I never understood what he meant and always just laughed politely.

Although I had always taken Andy's visits to my house for granted, I came home from school one afternoon to be told by my mother that Andy would be taking me and a friend, Billy Jones, to the Echo offices to meet the legendary 'Aunty Joan", and that we would be featured in Aunty Joan's Corner and even have our photograph in the paper. I was so excited and felt like a celebrity and could not understand why Billy Jones did not feel the same. He was like that, not really interested in anything.

Although my visit to the Liverpool Daily Post and Echo offices was the highlight of my week, the thing I remember mostly was the story Andy told me on our journey in to town.

"I had a very good friend," he said, quite nonchalantly, "he also worked at the Daily Post and Echo. He was worse than me." Andy paused and wiped a tear from his cheek. "He loved his job with all the people, asking them what they wanted." Andy stopped again, and looked vacantly through the window of the bus at the passing traffic. "I don't know how he died – I think he had pneumonia. He collapsed in the print room." Andy went right off the subject and began talking about something else. By now I was beginning to realise that he was not like other people and that I had to leave him to his own thoughts.

We travelled in silence until the bus had nearly reached Victoria Street. My friend, Billy Jones did not seem interested in what Andy was talking about and anyway I felt a little nervous being in town. Andy suddenly blurted: "My friend is always there." He lit the stump of a cigarette, something he always did. "You see, he loved his work and he still calls in to see what everyone wants." Andy's friend was also an errand boy and together they used to fetch drinks and sandwiches for the hundreds of staff at the main branch of the Liverpool newspaper.

My friend and I met Aunty Joan and then we had our photographs taken before wending our way through town to get the bus home.

"What was your friend's name?" I asked, the question, having been on my mind all this time.

"Jimmy," answered Andy quickly. "They called him Jimmy Green Teeth!" He walked on ahead, his head held low and his shoulders hunched in Andy's familiar way. "Jimmy Green Teeth."

"I thought that was your name," I retorted, realising what I had said. "I thought they called you Jimmy Green Teeth."

Andy stopped in the middle of the pavement, people hastily making their way home, pushing him from the side and shoving him from behind. "My friend was Jimmy Green Teeth. He collapsed and died in the print room. He's always there and always will be there."

I knew not to ask Andy any more questions and we climbed on the bus and made our way home, without another word being spoken about Andy's friend, Jimmy Green Teeth.

I later found out that the name Jimmy Green Teeth was a derogatory name given to people with learning difficulties in the 1940s and 50s. Andy's friend became known as the ghost of the Liverpool Daily Post and Echo and had been seen in the Victoria Street depot right up until the paper moved to its present premises in Old Hall Street.

I wonder where Jimmy Green Teeth is now, and if he ever moved to the new offices? Although no one has seen him in Old Hall Street, it doesn't mean to say he isn't there, taking the orders, checking that everyone is alright, does it?

56

GHOST HUNTER AND NEW ORLEANS

The most exciting work I have ever been involved in was being invited by Sony to feature in a documentary to promote their new Playstation 2 Game, Ghost Hunter, filmed on location in New Orleans.

The actual game was about a retired policeman who hunted evil spirits. His mission was to capture and destroy the malevolent entities who had occupied a World War Two battleship, a plantation house, and a graveyard deep within the Louisiana swamps. The weird thing was, during their research, the game makers discovered that there were real locations that replicated those on the game and these were also plagued by similar mischievous if not evil spirits.

My job was to visit the haunted location and meet the very disruptive entities face to face, just like the policeman on the game. Because of my musical background I had always wanted to go to New Orleans and so this was an ideal opportunity to kill two birds with one stone, so to speak. Little did I know that nearly everywhere in New Orleans is haunted by one thing or another and so I did have my work cut out.

I must admit, there was something quite magical about New Orleans, and I was very fortunate to visit it before it was nearly destroyed by the horrendous hurricane.

The first haunted location was the Second World War battleship, now in a dry dock museum on the Gulf of Mexico. It had been sunk in the war by Japanese bombers and had sustained hundreds of fatalities. The ship had been rescued from its Pacific Ocean grave and was now visited by thousands of tourists, completely oblivious to the fact that they were being watched by many ghostly eyes.

Accompanied by New Orleans parapsychologist Kalila Smith, armed with her ghost busting apparatus, we scoured the decks and boiler room in search for the alleged ghosts. I found this location extremely oppressive and was quite unnerved by the shadowy forms and light anomalies in the boiler room.

Apart from those phenomena I came face to face with a very angry naval officer standing on the upper deck, completely unaware that he was in fact dead. I was quite glad when we left the ship to head to our second destination, the plantation house in New Orleans.

The alleged haunted plantation house was the one featured on the label of a well known liquor bottle, Southern Comfort, and although it was originally on the banks of the Mississippi River, it is now surrounded by a stretch of barren land with some trees strategically grown to protect the old house from the intense and relentless sunlight. In fact, the plantation house was an ideal setting for an American Civil War movie, and was also only a stone's throw from the house featured in the classic movie Gone With The Wind.

On the Playstation Game the ghost hunter goes in search of an evil ghostly child, Milly Planter, and this house was allegedly haunted by a similar figure. We spent the entire day going over the house with a psychic fine tooth comb, and as soon as night descended the little girl came out to play! Although a mischievous spirit, I can't say she was evil and we did have lots of fun with her during our stay there.

Lights turned on and off by themselves, cameras worked when they were not connected to a power source and strange lights appeared on electrical cables when there was no electricity running through them.

A young slave girl had apparently been badly treated on the

plantation and had allegedly taken out her revenge by poisoning the owner's wife and children. Although we did not encounter the slave girl we did receive quite a lot of evidential communication from the wife who had been poisoned.

The old plantation house appeared to be 'alive' with all different kinds of paranormal activity, but for me the most interesting phenomenon was when the old rocking chair on the porch rocked backwards and forwards by itself, and Kalila and I both saw the ghostly figure of an old lady sitting contentedly on it. The last haunted location in New Orleans was by far the most frightening, for me at least. This was a ghostly graveyard deep within the Louisiana swamps that was said to be haunted by German settlers who had been cursed by a voodoo queen called Julia Brown.

I could not believe how beautifully picturesque it was as our boat chugged its way through the moss-covered water of the swamps, looked upon by the curious eyes of alligators and slithering water snakes. Our little motor-powered boat pushed its way for several miles down the river before we eventually reached our destination – Julia Brown's graveyard. It was only when we arrived there that the producer informed me that we would have to remain there until nightfall when I would have to wander alone in the graveyard with only a camera man to keep me company. I was terrified, not because of the ghostly atmosphere but because of the snakes and huge, jumping, very venomous spiders that seemed to be everywhere. Although I was assured by our guides that the spiders would not be interested in me, I was NOT convinced.

German cabbage growers had apparently settled in the swamps, not far from the home of Julia Brown, the voodoo queen. They were not nice to the eccentric woman, who placed a curse on them by saying they would all be killed by a hurricane.

Coincidence or not, the German settlers' village was destroyed, as Julia Brown had predicted, and no one survived except a young girl and an elderly black man. As the original curse included the young girl and the elderly man, they too eventually met an untimely death in freak accidents and it said that even today the families of both are still plagued with bad luck.

The night descended and I was left to my own devices. "Take one," the producer called and, as instructed, followed by the cameraman, I slowly and very carefully wended my way between the wooden crosses marking the positions of the graves. It was an ideal setting for such a programme. The owl hooted and wild dogs howled, and the cacophony of ghostly swamp sounds sent a shiver through my sweat-soaked body, as I walked deeper into the eerie graveyard.

The producer called: "Stop by that grave and say what you feel."

I just wanted to get the whole thing over and get out of this god-forsaken place. I immediately began to say what I psychically felt, and as I was speaking I heard the film crew gasp as they watched me from the safety of the gate to the graveyard.

Although I wondered what the matter was, it wasn't until we had finished filming and were ready to vacate the swamps that they told me a huge white owl had hovered for a few seconds above my head. In Native American culture this is quite ominous and really worried me all the time I was in New Orleans. In fact the portentous owl is believe to herald impending doom and disaster and so I was, quite understandably, quite relieved to leave New Orleans and return home to the UK.

Apart from the phenomenon of the owl, we also witnessed ghostly figures of light floating amidst the trees and intense light anomalies in the thick undergrowth. This graveyard in was by far the most frightening location on my visit to New Orleans and most certainly one I will never forget.

MY CONCLUSION

I have been working as a professional stage psychic and medium for over 25 years and have performed in some of the largest theatres in the UK, as well as appearing on television all over the world.

I have also worked with and known some of the greatest mediums of all time and I'm proud to say that they were my friends. I worked with the famous Doris Stokes on numerous occasions and, in fact, she officially opened my psychic centre, The Thought Workshop (as it was called) in Rodney Street in 1984.

World-renowned trance medium, spiritual teacher and best selling author Ursula Roberts visited my centre in 1986, as did international psychic artist Ivor James. In fact, Ivor visited the centre several times over the years.

Unfortunately, these people are now deceased but their names still live on to this day, in the absolutely brilliant work they did all over the world.

As well as working as a medium, I also lecture on the paranormal and metaphysics in colleges and universities worldwide. I have a very special interest in the so-called 'haunted house phenomenon', as well as in metaphysics and other paranormal subjects and so, unlike many other 'ghost story tellers', I can say that I have been involved with many of the stories in this book or extensively researched them.

No one could ever accuse me of leading an uneventful life – far from it. Whether I am in the cellar at the Slaughterhouse pub in Liverpool or in a ghostly graveyard in the Louisiana swamps, my work is never boring and presents me with something different every day.

About the Author

Billy Roberts has been psychic since he was a child and has been a professional stage medium for over 25 years.

Today he travels all over the world with his psychic stage shows, seminars and workshops, and is regarded as one of the UK's leading authorities on the paranormal. He appears regularly on television in the UK and abroad and has also presented his own Channel One television series entitled Secrets of the Paranormal.

He is the author of 11 books and has been featured in a documentary to promote Sony's Playstation 2 game Ghost Hunter, filmed on location in New Orleans.

Billy was the founder of The Thought Workshop, the UK's first centre for psychic and spiritual studies and alternative therapies, in Rodney Street, Liverpool, and also established The Billy Roberts Paranormal Study Centre in Penny Lane.

Billy has presented a series of four videos entitled Billy Roberts Investigates the Paranormal, in which he visited some of the North West's most haunted locations.

Billy has been personally involved in many of the stories in this book and extensively researched the others.

If you have a ghostly story to tell, contact Billy Roberts at www.billyroberts.co.uk